SOUPS, STARTERS AND SAVOURIES

Consultant Editor
Bridget Jones

WARD LOCK

A WARD LOCK BOOK

First published in the UK 1994
by Ward Lock
A Cassell Imprint
Villiers House
41/47 Strand
LONDON
WC2N 5JE

Editor: Jenni Fleetwood
Designer: Anne Fisher
Cover artwork by Angela Barnes
Inside artwork by Kevin Jones Associates

Distributed in the United States
by Sterling Publishing Co., Inc.
387 Park Avenue South, New York, NY 10016-8810

Distributed in Australia
by Capricorn Link (Australia) Pty Ltd
P.O. Box 665, Lane Cove, NSW 2066

British Library Cataloguing in Publication Data
The CIP data for this book is available
upon application to the British Library

ISBN 0-7063-7183-6

Typeset by Litho Link Ltd, Welshpool, Powys, Wales
Printed and bound in Spain by Cronion S.A. Barcelona

**Mrs Beeton's is a registered trademark
of Ward Lock Ltd**

CONTENTS

USEFUL WEIGHTS AND MEASURES

USING METRIC OR IMPERIAL MEASURES

Throughout the book, all weights and measures are given first in metric, then in Imperial. For example 100 g/4 oz, 150 ml/¼ pint or 15 ml/1 tbsp.

When following any of the recipes use either metric or Imperial – do not combine the two sets of measures as they are not interchangeable.

Weights The following chart lists some of the Metric/Imperial weights that are used in the recipes.

METRIC	IMPERIAL
15 g	½ oz
25 g	1 oz
50 g	2 oz
75 g	3 oz
100 g	4 oz
150 g	5 oz
175 g	6 oz
200 g	7 oz
225 g	8 oz
250 g	9 oz
275 g	10 oz
300 g	11 oz
350 g	12 oz
375 g	13 oz
400 g	14 oz
425 g	15 oz
450 g	1 lb
575 g	1¼ lb
675 g	1½ lb
800 g	1¾ lb
900 g	2 lb
1 kg	2¼ lb
1.4 kg	3 lb
1.6 kg	3½ lb
1.8 kg	4 lb
2.25 kg	5 lb

Liquid Measures Millilitres (ml), litres and fluid ounces (fl oz) or pints are used.

METRIC	IMPERIAL
50 ml	2 fl oz
125 ml	4 fl oz
150 ml	¼ pint
300 ml	½ pint
450 ml	¾ pint
600 ml	1 pint

Spoon Measures Both metric and Imperial equivalents are given for all spoon measures, expressed as millilitres and teaspoons (tsp) or tablespoons (tbsp).

All spoon measures refer to British standard measuring spoons and the quantities given are always for level spoons.

Do not use ordinary kitchen cutlery instead of proper measuring spoons as they will hold quite different quantities.

METRIC	IMPERIAL
1.25 ml	¼ tsp
2.5 ml	½ tsp
5 ml	1 tsp
15 ml	1 tbsp

Length All linear measures are expressed in millimetres (mm), centimetres (cm) or metres (m) and inches or feet. The following list gives examples of typical conversions.

METRIC	IMPERIAL
5 mm	¼ inch
1 cm	½ inch
2.5 cm	1 inch
5 cm	2 inches
15 cm	6 inches
30 cm	12 inches (1 foot)

OVEN TEMPERATURES

Three alternatives are used: degrees Celsius (°C), degrees Fahrenheit (°F) and gas. The settings given are for conventional ovens. If you have a fan oven, adjust the temperature according to the manufacturer's instructions.

°C	°F	GAS
110	225	¼
120	250	½
140	275	1
150	300	2
160	325	3
180	350	4
190	375	5
200	400	6
220	425	7
230	450	8
240	475	9

MICROWAVE INFORMATION

The information given is for microwave ovens rated at 650-700 watts.

The following terms have been used for the microwave settings: High, Medium, Defrost and Low. For each setting, the power input is as follows: High = 100% power, Medium = 50% power, Defrost = 30% power and Low = 20% power.

All microwave notes and timings are for guidance only: always read and follow the manufacturer's instructions for your particular appliance. Remember to avoid putting any metal in the microwave and never operate the microwave empty.

NOTES FOR AMERICAN READERS

In America the standard 8 oz cup measure is used. When translating pints, and fractions of pints, remember that the U.S. pint is equal to 16 fl oz or 2 cups, whereas the Imperial pint is 20 fl oz.

Equivalent metric/American measures

METRIC/IMPERIAL	AMERICAN
Weights	
450 g/1 lb butter or margarine	2 cups (4 sticks)
100 g/4 oz grated cheese	1 cup
450 g/1 lb flour	4 cups
450 g/1 lb granulated sugar	2 cups
450 g/1 lb icing sugar	3½ cups confectioners' sugar
200 g/7 oz raw long-grain rice	1 cup
100 g/4 oz cooked long-grain rice	1 cup
100 g/4 oz fresh white breadcrumbs	2 cups

Liquid Measures

METRIC/IMPERIAL	AMERICAN
150 ml/¼ pint	⅔ cup
300 ml/½ pint	1¼ cups
450 ml/¾ pint	2 cups
600 ml/1 pint	2½ cups
900 ml/1½ pints	3¾ cups
1 litre/1¾ pints	4 cups (2 U.S. pints)

Terminology Some useful American equivalents or substitutes for British ingredients are listed below:

BRITISH	AMERICAN
aubergine	eggplant
bicarbonate of soda	baking soda
biscuits	cookies, crackers
broad beans	fava or lima beans
chicory	endive
cling film	plastic wrap
cornflour	cornstarch
courgettes	zucchini
cream, single	cream, light
cream, double	cream, heavy
flour, plain	flour, all-purpose
frying pan	skillet
grill	broiler
minced meat	ground meat
prawn	shrimp
shortcrust pastry	basic pie dough
spring onion	scallion
sultana	golden raisin
swede	rutabaga

INTRODUCTION

This book sets out to provide alternative ideas for everyday light meals and snacks as well as a good range of recipes for first courses and special-occasion savouries. The opening section explains the role of nutrients in the diet and how they work to maintain a healthy body. This essential background to eating as a whole is especially relevant when considering the 'lesser' meals – those quick lunches or suppertime-snacks.

A healthy eating regime is often destroyed by poorly balanced light meals and snacks. In many respects it is easier to create a well-balanced main meal, focusing the menu on a variety of vegetables with an ample portion of carbohydrate and a well-chosen protein dish than it is to plan a nutritious light meal or snack. It is all too easy to fall into the trap of regularly eating a fairly unhealthy snack lunch; for example, a buttery sandwich with a high-fat filling, complemented by a packet of crisps and rounded off with a confectionery bar.

Many popular bought prepared dishes and ready-meals are highly processed, sometimes with a heavy fat content, and they often provide very little in the way of fibre. Although there is nothing wrong with eating such foods occasionally – and there is no denying that ready-prepared items are a real boon for the busy family – it is a mistake to rely on them for all other than the main meals of the day.

The recipes in this book are useful for a variety of occasions. Soups, in particular, are versatile and easy to prepare, with many being suitable for freezing. The first recipe chapter covers light soups for first courses, lunch or supper, then the following section moves on to include more substantial combinations which make hearty main meals. There are plenty of suggestions for accompaniments, with a later chapter in the book providing recipes for breads and crackers, many of which are ideal for batch baking and freezing. Slightly more substantial dishes which are practical to prepare for everyday suppers are also featured.

Even the most imaginative cooks occasionally need a little inspiration or new ideas for the opening course of a meal. There are light recipes ranging from dips and salads to pâtés and terrines, followed by an interesting range of hot dishes. Certain recipes are ideal for cooking ahead while others are quick to prepare at the last minute.

Rounding off a meal with a savoury is an old British tradition which is recalled in one of the feature spreads, with sample recipes to illustrate the types of foods which were served at the Victorian table and suggestions for including them or their modern counterparts in the contemporary menu.

Throughout the book, the emphasis is on adopting a broad-minded approach to healthy eating, with advice on balancing the occasional use of rich ingredients for special starters by concentrating on including plenty of vegetables, fruit and high-fibre foods in everyday snacks and meals. Alternative ingredients are included in many recipes which make use of high-fat foods, such as cream, and nutrition notes complement the food values to offer reminders on a variety of topics, from cooking methods to serving suggestions.

NUTRITION AND DIET

A basic understanding of nutrition leads to an awareness of the food we eat in relation to its use by the body and, consequently, to an appreciation of the importance of eating a balanced diet.

Food is the essential fuel for life, maintaining the body as well as building and repairing it. Foods are made up of a combination of different nutrients and, as the body digests the food, these nutrients are released and utilized. General guidelines are provided regarding the nutritional needs of the population; however, individual requirements vary. Factors that influence any one person's dietary needs include gender, age, build, lifestyle and health.

BALANCED DIET

A balanced diet provides all the essential nutrients and sufficient energy to meet an individual's needs and to maintain a healthy body weight without causing obesity. In young people, the diet must also include sufficient nutrients to sustain growth. Nutritional requirements relating to pregnancy, lactation, illness and special conditions should be provided by a doctor and/or dietician.

A balanced diet should include a wide selection of different types of foods, prepared and cooked in a variety of ways. Fresh foods and 'whole' foods are important in providing a balanced variety of nutrients. Raw and lightly cooked fruit and vegetables are also essential.

In general terms, the carbohydrate and vegetable content of the diet should dominate the protein and fat. A diet that lacks carbohydrate, fruit and vegetables is likely to have too high a fat content and to be lacking in fibre. Fibre, from vegetable and cereal sources, is also a vital ingredient for a balanced diet.

BASIC GUIDE TO NUTRIENTS

Protein
Used by the body for growth and repair, protein foods are composed of amino acids, in various amounts and combinations according to the food. There are eight specific amino acids which are an essential part of an adult's diet as they cannot be manufactured by the body from other foods; an additional one is necessary for young children, to sustain their rapid growth. In addition, nine other amino acids are widely available in protein foods, although a high intake of these is not vital as the human body can manufacture them if they are not adequately supplied by the diet.

The quality of any one protein food is determined by the number and proportion of amino acids it contains. Animal foods have a higher biological value than vegetable foods because they provide all the essential amino acids. Generally, no single vegetable food provides all the essential amino acids and they are not present in the proportions best suited to the human body. There are, however, important exceptions to this rule; certain non-animal foods are excellent sources of protein, notably soya beans, some types of nut and mycoprotein (quorn). Other beans and pulses, nuts and cereals are also excellent sources of good-quality protein. Since the amino acid content of vegetable foods varies, by mixing different foods and eating them in sufficient amounts, the necessary types and quantities of amino acids may be obtained.

As amino acids are not stored in a digestible form in the body, a regular supply is essential. This is most easily obtained from a mixture of animal and vegetable sources; if fish, poultry and meat are not eaten, then it is vital that a broad selection of vegetable sources and dairy foods are included to provide sufficient quantities of amino acids.

Carbohydrates

These are the energy-giving foods and may be divided into two main categories: starches and sugars. Starch is obtained from vegetables, cereals, some nuts and under-ripe bananas; sugar is found in fruit (including ripe bananas), honey, molasses and cane sugar.

Carbohydrates in the form of starch, known as complex carbohydrates, should form a significant proportion of the diet. For example, they should be eaten in larger quantities than protein foods, such as meat, poultry and fish. The sugar content of the diet should be limited.

If the diet is deficient in carbohydrates, the body will break down other foods to supply energy, eventually including proteins which have a more valuable role to play.

Fibre

At one time referred to as roughage, fibre is a complex carbohydrate which is not totally digested and absorbed by the body; however, it is vital as a carrier of moisture and waste products through the digestive system.

Fibre is obtained from cereals and vegetables. Good sources are wholegrain rice, oats, wholemeal flour and its products. Sources of vegetable fibre include beans and pulses, some types of fruit, as well as vegetables.

Raw and lightly cooked foods (where appropriate) generally provide more fibre than well-cooked foods; similarly more refined foods offer less fibre than wholefoods and unrefined ingredients.

Fats

Fat and oils provide energy as well as being important sources of certain vitamins and fatty acids. They may be loosely divided into saturated fats and unsaturated fats. Unsaturated fats may be further grouped into polyunsaturated and monounsaturated, depending on their chemical compositions. Although the majority of fatty foods contain both saturated and unsaturated fats, as a general rule animal sources have a higher proportion of saturated fats and vegetable sources are richer in unsaturates.

The recommended fat intake is calculated as a percentage of the total energy value of the diet. The energy value (in calories or joules) of fat eaten should be no more than 35% of the total energy intake with the major proportion of fat in the diet being the unsaturated type.

It is important to remember that young children (under five years of age) should not follow low-fat diets. Although their meals should not contain high proportions of fatty foods (fried foods, chips, high-fat snacks), their fat intake should not be limited by the use of skimmed milk, low-fat cheese and so on.

Vitamins

Although each of the vitamins has specific functions within the body, they also play vital roles in regulating metabolism, helping to repair tissues and assisting in the conversion of carbohydrates and fats into energy. Vitamin deficiency results in general poor health as well as certain specific illnesses.

Vitamins fall into two groups; fat-soluble and water-soluble. Fat-soluble vitamins include A, D, E and K; water-soluble vitamins include C and B-group vitamins. Fat-soluble vitamins can be stored by the body, whereas any excess of the water-soluble type is passed out. This means that a regular supply of water-soluble vitamins is essential and that an excess is unlikely to be harmful. Conversely, the fat-soluble vitamins which are stored in the body should not be consumed to excess as this can result in a condition known as hypervitaminosis. It is important to remember that an excess can be dangerous when taking vitamin supplements, or when eating a very high proportion of foods which are particularly rich in any one (or more) of the fat-soluble vitamins.

Vitamin A Found in fish liver oils, liver, kidney, dairy produce and eggs, vitamin A is important to prevent night blindness. It also contributes to the general health of the eyes and to the condition of the skin. Carotene, found in carrots and yellow or dark green vegetables such as peppers and spinach, can be converted into vitamin A in the body.

If the diet is excessively rich in vitamin A, or supplements are taken for a prolonged period, it is possible for stores to build up to toxic levels in the human liver.

B-group Vitamins This is a large group of water-soluble vitamins, linked because of their importance and use in the body. They play vital roles in promoting chemical reactions, in the release of energy from food and in the efficient functioning of the nervous system. They are essential for general good health and deficiency diseases occur comparatively quickly if these vitamins are missing from the diet.

Thiamin (vitamin B1), riboflavin (vitamin B2), vitamin B12, vitamin B6 (pyridoxine), nicotinic acid, folate, pantothenic acid and biotin are all included in this group (or complex) and each has its own particular characteristics.

In general, meat, offal, dairy produce, and cereals are good sources of B-group vitamins. Some of these vitamins are destroyed by prolonged cooking, notably thiamin, and long exposure to sunlight destroys riboflavin which is found in milk. Refined flour and bread are fortified with thiamin to meet natural levels in comparable wholemeal products. Breakfast cereals are also enriched with, or naturally rich in, B-group vitamins.

Vitamin C or Ascorbic Acid A water-soluble vitamin, this cannot be stored in the body, therefore a regular supply is essential. The main function of this vitamin is to maintain healthy connective tissue (the cell-structure within the body) and healthy blood. It also plays an important role in the healing of wounds. A deficiency can lead to susceptibility to infections.

Vitamin C is found in fresh and frozen vegetables, notably peppers and green vegetables, and in fruit, particularly blackcurrants and citrus fruit. Many fruit juices and drinks are fortified with vitamin C. Potatoes are also a valuable supply; although they are not a rich source, when eaten regularly and in quantity they make an important contribution to a healthy diet.

Vitamin C is the most easily destroyed of all vitamins and may be affected by light, heat, staleness, exposure to air and overcooking. The vitamin is also destroyed by alkaline substances, such as bicarbonate of soda.

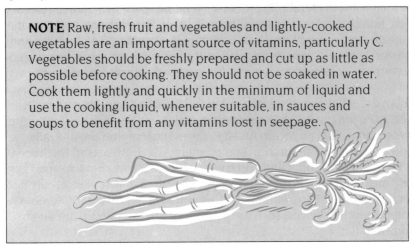

NOTE Raw, fresh fruit and vegetables and lightly-cooked vegetables are an important source of vitamins, particularly C. Vegetables should be freshly prepared and cut up as little as possible before cooking. They should not be soaked in water. Cook them lightly and quickly in the minimum of liquid and use the cooking liquid, whenever suitable, in sauces and soups to benefit from any vitamins lost in seepage.

Vitamin D Essential in promoting calcium absorption, a deficiency will result in an inadequate supply of calcium being made available for building and repairing bones and teeth. A diet which is too rich in vitamin D can result in excessive calcium absorption and storage which can be damaging, so supplements should only be taken on medical advice.

Vitamin D is manufactured by the body from the action of sunlight on the skin – this is the primary source for most adults. The vitamin is naturally present in cod liver oil and oily fish such as herrings, mackerel, salmon and sardines. Eggs contain vitamin D, and it can also be manufactured from vegetable sources. Some foods, such as margarine, are fortified with vitamin D.

Vitamin E This vitamin is found in small amounts in most foods and the better sources include vegetable oils, eggs and cereals (especially wheatgerm).

Its role in the body is not clearly established, although unsubstantiated claims are made about its contribution to fertility and its role in improving circulation.

Vitamin K Widely found in vegetables and cereals, this vitamin can be manufactured in the body. Vitamin K contributes towards normal blood clotting. Deficiency is rare, due to a ready supply being available in a mixed diet.

A broad mixed diet, including plenty of raw and lightly cooked fruit and vegetables as well as animal and dairy foods, is likely to provide an adequate supply of vitamins. The value of fresh foods, dairy produce, bread and cereals is obvious. Deficiency can occur in restricted diets where meat and poultry are not eaten and corresponding levels of vitamins are not taken from dairy products or cereals. Those following a vegan diet are most vulnerable, and a diet free of animal products is not recommended.

Minerals

Minerals and trace elements are essential for a healthy body as they play important roles in metabolic processes relating to to the nervous system, glands, muscle control and the supply of water. They are only required in minute quantities and a well balanced diet containing plenty of fresh and whole foods should provide an adequate supply. Mineral supplements should only be taken on medical advice as overdoses can upset metabolism.

Iron An essential constituent of red blood cells and important in muscles, iron can be stored in the body. The diet must maintain the store as, if it becomes depleted, anaemia can result. An adequate supply of iron is especially important during menstruation and pregnancy, as both use up the iron supply.

Found in meat, offal and green vegetables, such as spinach, and eggs, the iron in meat and offal is the most readily absorbed; it is less easily utilized from vegetable sources. The availability of vitamin C is important to promote iron absorption; other factors, such as the presence of tannin, can impair absorption.

Calcium Important in building and maintaining healthy teeth and bones, as well as for normal blood clotting, muscle function and a healthy nervous system, calcium is obtained from milk, cheese, bread, fortified flour and vegetables. The calcium found in milk and dairy produce is likely to be more easily absorbed than that in green vegetables or whole grains (although the system can adjust to utilizing the mineral from less ready sources) and an adequate supply of vitamin D is necessary for efficient calcium absorption.

Phosphorus Along with calcium, this is valuable for bones and teeth. It is widely distributed in food and deficiency is unknown in man.

Potassium, Chlorine and Sodium These play an important role in the balance of body fluids and they are essential for muscle and nerve function. Sodium and chlorine are added to food in the form of salt; sodium is found naturally in meat and milk, and it is added to bread, cereal products and manufactured foods. Potassium is found naturally in meat, vegetables and milk.

Trace Elements These are required by the body in very small amounts and include iodine, fluorine, magnesium, zinc, manganese, cobalt, selenium, molybdenum and chromium. An adequate supply of trace elements is almost always found in the diet and deficiency is extremely rare. Unprescribed supplements should be avoided as they can be detrimental to health.

SPECIFIC NEEDS

Most people have particular dietary needs at some time during their life, if only as babies or young children.

Babies
Breast milk is the ideal food for young babies as it provides all the nutrients they require for the first few months of life. Even if this method of feeding is not continued in the long term, it is a very good idea to breast-feed a baby for the first few days, as valuable antibodies are passed from the mother to help the baby fight infection in the early months.

Bottle-fed babies should be given one of the manufactured milk formulas. These should be prepared exactly according to the manufacturer's instructions or according to the health visitor's or doctor's advice.

Regular checks on the baby's progress are important and any problems should be brought to professional attention immediately.

The weaning process varies from infant to infant; however, between the ages of four to six months a baby should be ready to try a little solid food. By eighteen months, the infant should be able to cope with a mixed diet based on adult foods, following general guidelines for balanced eating. Milk is still an important supplement during this time of rapid growth.

Toddlers and Young Children
Fads and eating difficulties are common in young children, who are too busy discovering the world around them to concentrate for the length of time necessary to learn about meals. Since toddlers and young children are quickly satisfied, it is important that they are introduced to good eating habits and that their meals are nutritious; sweet or fatty snacks are to be avoided and bread, milk, vegetables, fruit, cheese and other valuable foods should be introduced. New foods should be presented in small amounts along with familiar ingredients. Milk is still an important source of nutrients, particularly for difficult eaters.

Providing a meal-time routine and making the process of eating a pleasure is all-important. Children should not be encouraged to play with food, but they should look forward to eating it. Small, frequent yet regular meals, are ideal: in theory, these occasions should be relaxed, free of distractions from the business of eating, and traumatic scenes relating to food rejection should be avoided.

School Children

Fast-growing and active children need a highly nutritious diet, so the substitution of sweets, fatty snacks, sweet drinks and sticky cakes for meals should be avoided. These types of foods should be rare treats.

Breakfasts and packed lunches need special attention. The first meal of the day should be nutritious and provide sufficient energy to keep the child on the move until lunchtime: bread, cereals and milk, eggs and fruit are all practical and useful foods. Raw vegetables, semi-sweet biscuits and crackers are practical mid-morning snack foods but they should not spoil the appetite for lunch. Packed lunches, if eaten, should contain a variety of foods – bread, salad vegetables, some form of protein and a piece of fruit. If a packed lunch is the norm, tea and an early supper are important meals.

As a general guide, every meal should provide growing children with a good balance of valuable nutrients, and additional milk drinks (whole or semi-skimmed) are excellent sources of the calcium which is so important for strong teeth and bones, as well as other nutrients. Sweet foods and confectionery should be avoided as they cause tooth decay and can lead to obesity; similarly, fatty cooking methods and high-fat foods should not be a regular feature in the diet. The importance of fibre, raw fruit and vegetables must be stressed.

Adolescents and Teenagers

This group also requires a highly nutritious, energy-packed diet, but unfortunately, young people are particularly prone to food fads and fashions and it can be difficult to get a teenager to eat a balanced diet. While it is essential to provide all the necessary nutrients, it is important to avoid obesity in this group. Reduced-calorie diets are not recommended, but over-eating must be controlled and the types of food eaten should be carefully monitored.

During this period of rapid growth and development, adopting an active lifestyle and participating in regular exercise is as important as eating well. Young people in this age group should be encouraged to take an interest in nutrition, food and the relationship between a balanced diet, health and fitness.

Parents should try to pass on an understanding of food shopping, meal planning and food preparation, together with an appreciation of the positive benefits of a good diet. This is particularly important for young people who are about to embark on their first experience of living alone and catering for themselves.

Pregnancy and Lactation

A woman should pay special attention to diet during pregnancy as she will need to provide sufficient nutrients and energy for her own needs as well as those of the growing baby. The nutritional requirements continue after birth and during lactation, when the mother is feeding the new baby. The doctor or clinic should provide dietary advice, recommending supplements as necessary.

The mother's responsibility is to ensure that her diet is varied, with emphasis on foods rich in minerals, vitamins and energy. Sweets, chocolates and foods which satisfy without offering nutritional benefit should be avoided in favour of fruit, vegetables, dairy produce, bread and protein foods.

Elderly People

Problems relating to nutrition and the elderly are often linked to social factors. The cost and effort of eating well can deter some elderly people from shopping for a variety of foods and therefore from cooking fresh ingredients. Although many elderly people are extremely active, others may have physical difficulty in shopping or spending long periods standing to prepare meals; in this case help should be sought with planning a practical diet. Equally, dental problems restrict some elderly people from eating well and these can, and should, be overcome by visiting a dentist.

Hot, solid meals are important, particularly in winter. Some elderly people get through the day by eating lots of snacks and this can be detrimental to health; cakes, biscuits and favourite puddings may be pleasant and comforting but they do not constitute a balanced diet. The appetite is often reduced, particularly as the person becomes less active, so meals that are small must contain a high proportion of valuable nutrients. Wholemeal bread, dairy products and cereals with milk are all practical snacks.

The pleasure often disappears from eating when meals are lonely occasions and the palate is not as efficient as it once was. Special centres and meal services exist and these should be used, not only by those who are prevented from cooking for themselves by physical limitations, but also by all who need the company and contact that such services offer.

All recipes (except stocks) include a guide to the content of key nutrients: protein, carbohydrate, fat and fibre.

- Where less rich alternatives are given for high-fat foods, the food values are based on the lighter ingredient. For example if an ingredients list includes either cream or fromage frais, the food values reflect the latter.
- Values are based on very low fat fromage frais where applicable.
- Total values and values per portion are provided. The values per portion relate to the number of servings suggested at the end of the recipe unless otherwise stated. Where a range of servings is given, the number used in the calculation is given in brackets at the top of the chart.
- Quantities are expressed in grammes (g) and rounded up to the nearest whole figure. Where a value is less than 1g, a dash indicates that the content of that nutrient is negligible in the context of this information.

FIRST COURSE SOUPS

MAKING SOUP

Making your own stock is still the best way to obtain a fine soup and it is essential if you intend serving a high-quality consommé; however, some bought stocks are of good quality. Bouillon cubes or chilled stocks can be a useful base for some soups, as can certain canned consommés. If a good-quality stock is not available, it is better to use water with additional flavouring ingredients such as celery, onions, carrots and parsley than to crumble in powerful stock cubes with poor flavour which may dominate the soup.

Tips for making stocks and soups
- Use good quality boiling or stewing cuts of meat, trimmings and bones for making stock. Trim off excess fat before you begin, and when the stock has cooled, skim off all surface fat.
- Leftovers from a roast give excellent flavour to stocks. For the richest flavour and a good dark stock, use uncooked bones. These should be roasted in the oven until well browned, then simmered with flavouring ingredients as described in the recipe for Rich Strong Stock. This method is not suitable for a light stock.
- Bones, cut or chopped into pieces, should be used whenever possible. (Ask the butcher to chop marrow bones.) However, on their own, bones do not give sufficient flavour, so use a meaty carcass or add some raw meat.
- To extract the maximum flavour, heat the ingredients gently and cook for long periods. Rapid boiling is not recommended except at the end of cooking, when it may be desirable to reduce and concentrate the stock.
- Do not add salt and pepper to stock at the beginning of cooking. The cooked stock should be seasoned according to the requirements of the finished dish and only after it has been reduced and concentrated as required. Remove scum as it rises to the surface of the stock.
- When making a meat stock, bring the water and meat trimmings to simmering point and skim the liquid before adding vegetables and other flavouring ingredients.
- Ask the fishmonger for bones and trimmings for making fish stock, but do not add gills, which can make the stock bitter.
- Use herbs and spices sparingly and balance strong and delicate flavours carefully.
- When the stock reaches the desired strength, allow it to cool, then strain it well. The stock may be clarified, see overleaf.
- Cool and chill stocks as quickly as possible after cooking and store them in the refrigerator for 1-2 days. Stock freezes well; to save space it may be further reduced and its flavour concentrated by boiling, but remember to label the pack with the estimated concentration. Reducing by half to three quarters is appropriate, depending on the original volume.

- Good beef or chicken stock can be made by substituting 450 g / 1 lb lean minced beef or 1 chicken quarter for stewing meat or bones. Add the same vegetables and flavouring ingredients as for Rich Strong Stock. The result will be a lighter stock; a practical solution to the problem of making authentic stock when a meaty carcass or the remains of a joint are not available.

Clarifying stock

Scald a saucepan (not aluminium), a piece of muslin, a metal sieve and a whisk. Pour the strained stock into the pan. Lightly whisk 2 egg whites and crush the washed shells from 2 eggs; add to the stock. Heat slowly to simmering point, whisking to form a thick white crust. Stop whisking, allow the stock to rise in the pan, then turn the heat off just before it boils. Repeat twice more. Line the sieve with the muslin and place it over a clean bowl. Strain the stock through the muslin. Try not to break the crust which acts as a filter.

White Stock

1.4 kg / 3 lb knuckle of veal
   on the bone, or other
   stewing veal
2 chicken drumsticks or
   poultry trimmings
1 onion, sliced
1 carrot, quartered
2 celery sticks, quartered
2 open cup mushrooms,
   quartered
1 bouquet garni
4 white peppercorn
1 blade of mace

Put the bones in a large saucepan. Add 900 ml / 1½ pints water. Bring to the boil, skim the surface, then add the remaining ingredients. Lower the heat and simmer for 30 minutes. Add a further 900 ml / 1½ pints water and simmer for about 3 hours more. Cool quickly, then strain. Skim off surface fat. Season and use as required.

MAKES ABOUT 1.5 LITRES / 2¾ PINTS

PRESSURE COOKER TIP

Meat and poultry stocks, made with raw or cooked meat and bones, can be prepared in the pressure cooker in approximately 40 minutes at 15 lb pressure. Follow the manufacturer's recommendations regarding the maximum quantity of ingredients and liquid for the pan; failing this, make a concentrated stock by reducing the volume of water to ensure that the pan is no more than half to two-thirds full. Add extra water and simmer briefly in the open pan after the pressure has been reduced.

Rich Strong Stock

This recipe makes a large quantity of stock which freezes well for future use. Although the quantities may be reduced, a large volume of liquid is required to cover marrow bones. It is more practical to invest in a large stockpot or saucepan and to boil a large quantity occasionally than to reduce the weight of ingredients in proportion to water to make a weaker meat stock.

675 g / 1½ lb shin of beef
  on the bone
675 g / 1½ lb knuckle of
  veal on the bone, or other
  stewing veal
450 g / 1 lb beef marrow
  bones
1 chicken drumstick or
  poultry trimmings
1 onion, sliced
1 carrot, quartered
100 g / 4 oz gammon or
  bacon, diced
1 small turnip, roughly
  chopped
2 celery sticks, quartered
2 open cup mushrooms,
  quartered
1 tomato, quartered
1 bouquet garni
4 white peppercorns
2 cloves
1 blade of mace

Set the oven at 200°C / 400°F / gas 6. Put the bones in a roasting tin and roast for about 2 hours until browned.

Transfer the bones to a large saucepan. Pour off the fat from the tin, add some boiling water and stir to scrape all the sediment off the tin. Then add to the bones in the pan. Add the onion and carrot.

Add about 5.6 litres / 10 pints water to cover the bones generously. Bring to the boil, skim the surface, then lower the heat and add the remaining ingredients. Simmer for about 5 hours. Cool, then strain. Skim off surface fat. Season and use as required.

MAKES ABOUT 5.3 LITRES / 9 PINTS

NUTRITION NOTE

Food values are not included for the stock recipes as they do not contain significant quantities of these nutrients.

Chicken Stock

4 *chicken drumsticks or 1*
   meaty chicken carcass
1 *small onion, sliced*
1 *carrot, roughly chopped*
1 *celery stick, sliced*
1 *bouquet garni*
5 ml / 1 *tsp white*
   peppercorns

Break or chop the carcass into manageable pieces.
Put the chicken in a large saucepan with 1.75 litres /
3 pints cold water. Bring to the boil, then skim any
scum off the surface.

Add the remaining ingredients, lower the heat and
simmer for 3-4 hours. Cool quickly, then strain.
Skim off surface fat. Season and use as required.

MAKES ABOUT 1.4 LITRES / 2½ PINTS

Vegetable Stock

Vary the vegetables according to the market selection
and your personal taste.

2 *onions, sliced*
2 *leeks, trimmed, sliced and*
   washed
1 *small turnip, chopped*
4 *celery sticks, sliced*
2 *tomatoes, chopped*
1 *bouquet garni*
6 *black peppercorns*
2 *cloves*
a few lettuce leaves
a few spinach leaves
a few watercress sprigs
2.5 ml / ½ *tsp yeast extract*
   (*optional*)
salt

Put the root vegetables, celery, tomatoes, herbs and
spices in a large saucepan. Add 2 litres / 3½ pints
water. Bring to the boil, lower the heat and simmer
for 1 hour.

Add the lettuce, spinach and watercress and
simmer for 1 hour more. Stir in the yeast extract, if
using, and add salt to taste. Strain and use as
required.

MAKES ABOUT 1.75 LITRES / 3 PINTS

Fish Stock

fish bones and trimmings without gills, which cause bitterness
5 ml / 1 tsp salt
1 small onion, sliced
2 celery sticks, sliced
4 white peppercorns
1 bouquet garni

Break up any bones and wash the fish trimmings, if used. Put the bones, trimmings or heads in a saucepan and cover with 1 litre / 1¾ pints cold water. Add the salt.

Bring the liquid to the boil and add the vegetables, peppercorns and bouquet garni. Lower the heat, cover and simmer gently for 30-40 minutes. Do not cook the stock for longer than 40 minutes or it may develop a bitter taste. Strain, cool quickly and use as required.

MAKES ABOUT 1 LITRE / 1¾ PINTS

VARIATION

White Wine Fish Stock Add 100 ml / 3½ fl oz dry white wine, 4-5 mushroom stalks and 1 sliced carrot. Simmer for 30 minutes only.

Lobster Bisque

Frozen lobster is ideal for making soup. It is important to boil the lobster trimmings and flesh in the wine for at least 3 minutes. The alcohol in the wine extracts much of the flavour from the lobster, vegetables and herbs.

FOOD VALUES	TOTAL	PER PORTION (4)
Protein	36g	9g
Carbohydrate	43g	11g
Fat	25g	6g
Fibre	4g	1g
kcals	608	152

shell, trimmings and a little of the flesh of 1 small or medium cooked lobster
1 onion, thinly sliced
1 carrot, thinly sliced
1 garlic clove, thinly sliced
1 bay leaf
1 blade of mace
5 ml / 1 tsp lemon juice
5 ml / 1 tsp anchovy essence
125 ml / 4 fl oz white wine
750 ml / 1¼ pints Fish Stock (page 21)
salt and pepper
15 ml / 1 tbsp cooked lobster coral (optional)
25 g / 1 oz butter
25 g / 1 oz plain flour
125 ml / 4 fl oz fromage frais

Crush the lobster shell and put it in a heavy-bottomed saucepan with the trimmings. Flake the flesh finely, setting a few neat pieces aside for the garnish. Add the remaining flesh to the pan with the onion, carrot and garlic. Put in the bay leaf, mace, lemon juice, anchovy essence and wine and bring to the boil. Cook briskly for 35 minutes. Add the fish stock and a little salt. Boil, lower the heat and simmer for 1 hour.

Strain the soup through a metal sieve into a large jug or bowl, rubbing through any pieces of firm lobster. Pound the lobster coral (if used) in a small bowl, then rub through a clean sieve into a second bowl. Set the coral aside.

Melt the butter in a saucepan and stir in the flour. Cook for 1 minute, stirring, then gradually add the strained soup. Bring to the boil, stirring constantly. Add the reserved lobster coral, stirring all the time.

Off the heat, add the fromage frais and the reserved lobster pieces, with salt and pepper, if required. Return the pan to the heat and warm through gently. Do not overheat the soup or the fromage frais will curdle. Serve at once.

SERVES 4 TO 6

Creamy Onion Soup

FOOD VALUES	TOTAL	PER PORTION (4)
Protein	24g	6g
Carbohydrate	85g	21g
Fat	32g	8g
Fibre	8g	1g
kcals	705	176

30 ml / 2 tbsp oil
4 large onions, finely
  chopped
50 g / 2 oz plain flour
1.1 litres / 2 pints White
  Stock (page 18)
salt and white pepper
1.25 ml / ¼ tsp ground
  mace
150 ml / ¼ pint fromage
  frais

Heat the oil in a large saucepan. Add the onions and stir well. Cover the pan and cook over gentle heat for 20 minutes until soft but not coloured.

Stir in the flour and cook for 1 minute, then gradually add the stock. Cook over moderate heat until the mixture boils and thickens. Season to taste with salt, pepper and mace. Simmer the soup, stirring occasionally, for about 30 minutes or until the onions are very tender and the soup is creamy.

In a small bowl, stir a little of the hot soup into the fromage frais, mix well, then add the contents of the bowl to the soup, stirring over the lowest heat for a few seconds until warmed through – do not allow the soup to simmer or the fromage frais will curdle. Serve at once.

SERVES 4 TO 6

23

Soup à la Flamande

FOOD VALUES	TOTAL	PER PORTION
Protein	43g	7g
Carbohydrate	133g	22g
Fat	24g	4g
Fibre	17g	3g
kcals	889	145

25 g / 1 oz butter
2 large onions, chopped
1 leek, trimmed, sliced and
   washed
8 celery sticks, thinly sliced
450 g / 1 lb potatoes, diced
1.1 litres / 2 pints Chicken
   Stock (page 20) or
   Vegetable Stock (page
   20)
salt and pepper
300 ml / ½ pint fromage
   frais

Melt the butter in a large saucepan. Add the onions, leek and celery and fry over gentle heat for about 10 minutes or until the onions and leeks are soft.

Stir in the potatoes and stock, bring to the boil, then lower the heat and simmer the soup for about 30 minutes or until the potatoes and celery are tender.

Purée the soup in a blender or food processor, or rub through a sieve into a clean pan. Add plenty of salt and pepper.

Stir in the fromage frais and heat through gently. Do not allow the soup to boil.

SERVES 6

Jerusalem Artichoke Soup

Unlike the globe artichoke, which grows above the ground, the Jerusalem artichoke is a tuber. It makes a delicious winter soup.

FOOD VALUES	TOTAL	PER PORTION
Protein	55g	9g
Carbohydrate	65g	11g
Fat	47g	8g
Fibre	4g	1g
kcals	884	147

15 ml / 1 tbsp oil
3 rindless back bacon slices, chopped
4 celery sticks, thinly sliced
1 small turnip, cubed
1 onion, chopped
1 kg / 2¼ lb Jerusalem artichokes, see Mrs Beeton's Tip
1.5 litres / 2¾ pints White Stock (page 18)
salt and pepper
cayenne pepper
300 ml / ½ pint reduced-fat single cream, plain yogurt or fromage frais

Heat the oil in a large saucepan. Add the bacon, celery, turnip and onion and fry over gentle heat for about 10 minutes until the vegetables are soft but not coloured.

Peel and cube the artichokes. Add them to the pan with the stock. Bring to the boil, lower the heat and simmer for about 15 minutes or until all the vegetables are tender.

Purée the soup in a blender or food processor, or rub through a sieve into a clean pan. Add salt, pepper and cayenne to taste. Stir in the cream, yogurt or fromage frais and reheat gently. Do not allow the soup to boil.

SERVES 6

MRS BEETON'S TIP

The flesh of Jerusalem artichokes discolours very rapidly, so prepare the vegetables only when required or put the cubes into water to which a little lemon juice or wine vinegar has been added.

Pumpkin Soup

FOOD VALUES	TOTAL	PER PORTION
Protein	22g	4g
Carbohydrate	41g	7g
Fat	33g	6g
Fibre	11g	2g
kcals	539	90

30 ml / 2 tbsp oil
1 onion, finely chopped
1 garlic clove, crushed
1 kg / 2¼ lb pumpkin,
   peeled, seeded and cubed
1.5 litres / 2¾ pints
   Chicken Stock (page 20)
   or Vegetable Stock (page
   20)
5 ml / 1 tsp ground
   coriander seeds
5 ml / 1 tsp ground
   cinnamon
2.5 ml / ½ tsp ground
   cumin
salt and pepper
150 ml / ¼ pint reduced-fat
   single cream or fromage
   frais

Heat the oil in a large saucepan, add the onion and garlic and cook over gentle heat for 10 minutes until soft but not coloured. Add the pumpkin cubes, stock and spices, with salt and pepper to taste. Bring to the boil, lower the heat and simmer for about 30 minutes or until the pumpkin is tender.

Purée the soup in a blender or food processor, or rub through a sieve into a clean pan. Taste and add more salt and pepper if required. The soup should be quite spicy. Reheat without boiling.

Ladle the soup into individual bowls and top each portion with a little cream or fromage frais.

SERVES 6

VARIATION

Pumpkin and Apple Soup Omit the coriander and cumin. Add 2 peeled, cored and sliced cooking apples with the pumpkin. Continue as above, then stir in a little sugar to taste when reheated. The sweetness should just balance the tang of the apples. Serve as above.

Cream of Lettuce Soup

FOOD VALUES	TOTAL	PER PORTION
Protein	23g	6g
Carbohydrate	64g	16g
Fat	24g	6g
Fibre	8g	2g
kcals	548	137

400 g / 14 oz lettuce,
  shredded
600 ml / 1 pint White Stock
  (page 18)
30 ml / 2 tbsp butter
1 onion, finely chopped
1 garlic clove, crushed
225 g / 8 oz potatoes, cubed
1 bouquet garni
salt and pepper
150 ml / ¼ pint fromage
  frais

Put the lettuce in a large heatproof bowl. Bring the stock to the boil in a deep saucepan, pour over the lettuce and set aside.

Melt the butter in the clean pan, add the onion, garlic, potatoes and bouquet garni, and fry over gentle heat, turning the vegetables frequently, for 10 minutes. Add the lettuce and stock. Stir in salt and pepper to taste. Bring to the boil, then lower the heat and simmer for 2 minutes or until the lettuce is tender.

Remove the bouquet garni. Purée the soup in a blender or food processor, or rub through a sieve into a clean pan. Reheat to simmering point, then remove the pan from the heat.

Mix the fromage frais with a little of the hot soup. Whisk the mixture into the remaining soup, return it to the heat and reheat without boiling, stirring all the time. Taste and adjust the seasoning, if necessary. Serve hot.

SERVES 4

Celery Soup

FOOD VALUES	TOTAL	PER PORTION
Protein	23g	6g
Carbohydrate	58g	15g
Fat	31g	8g
Fibre	14g	4g
kcals	586	146

15 ml / 1 tbsp oil
1 head of celery, finely sliced
2 leeks, trimmed, sliced and washed
1 small potato, diced
1 litre / 1¾ pints White Stock (page 18)
salt and pepper
grated nutmeg
300 ml / ½ pint milk

Heat the oil in a large saucepan. Add the celery and leeks and cook over gentle heat for 10 minutes until soft.

Add the potato and stock. Bring to the boil, then lower the heat and simmer for 20 minutes or until the vegetables are tender. Purée the soup in a blender or food processor, or rub through a sieve into a clean pan. Add salt, pepper and nutmeg to taste. Return the soup to the heat and simmer for 10 minutes. Finally stir in the milk and heat through before serving.

SERVES 4

MRS BEETON'S TIP

Celery seeds may be used to flavour soup. They are very small and pale green-beige in colour. Pound them to a powder in a mortar, using a pestle, then add to potato soup or other plain vegetable soups.

Cream of Almond Soup

The delicate flavour of this soup makes it the perfect introduction to a simple summer meal.

FOOD VALUES	TOTAL	PER PORTION (4)
Protein	45g	11g
Carbohydrate	53g	13g
Fat	76g	19g
Fibre	6g	2g
kcals	1064	266

300 ml / ½ pint milk
pared rind of 1 lemon
25 g / 1 oz butter
25 g / 1 oz plain flour
1 litre / 1¾ pints Chicken
   Stock (page 20)
salt and pepper
75 g / 3 oz ground almonds
pinch of cayenne pepper
2.5 ml / ½ tsp ground mace
175 ml / 6 fl oz fromage frais

Place the milk and lemon rind in a saucepan. Bring to just below boiling point, then remove the pan from the heat.

Melt the butter in a saucepan, stir in the flour and cook for 2 minutes. Gradually add the stock, stirring all the time, then continue to cook until the mixture boils and thickens. Add salt and pepper to taste.

Remove from the heat. Gradually stir in the milk mixture. When the mixture is smooth and creamy, add the ground almonds, cayenne, mace and fromage frais. Heat very gently without allowing the soup to simmer as this will cause it to curdle. Remove the lemon rind and serve.

SERVES 4 TO 6

GARNISHES AND ACCOMPANIMENTS FOR SOUP

As the first course of a meal, soup should make a positive impression, whetting the appetite for the other dishes to follow. Soups served as starters should not be too filling and the portions should not be too large.

Unfortunately, the colour and texture of some puréed soups can be rather uninspiring, despite the fact that their flavour is superb. As well as using garnishes to improve the appearance of the soup, it is important to offer accompaniments which provide a pleasing contrast in texture.

Opting to lighten creamy soups by using fromage frais, plain yogurt or a reduced-fat cream makes a positive contribution to the menu when planning a meal of three or more courses. Although there is no need to exclude cream completely from the diet, it can be a mistake to serve a rich soup for the first course of a special-occasion meal, especially if you intend making a luscious dessert. When planning dinner-party menus, it is worth remembering that as everyday diets have become lighter, many people feel quite uncomfortable if they eat a very rich meal.

GARNISHES FOR SOUP

Creamy Swirls As well as cream, fromage frais or plain yogurt may be swirled into smooth, thickened soups. Since most types of fromage frais and yogurt are too thick to pour, stir in a little milk to give the required pouring consistency. Use a small jug or large spoon to swirl the cream, fromage frais or yogurt into the soup.

Chopped Herbs Chopped parsley or snipped chives are versatile as they complement most flavours; otherwise select a herb which is used in the soup or one which mirrors the main ingredient. Sprinkle the herbs over individual portions just before taking them to the table.

MRS BEETON'S TIP

A quick way of chopping a small amount of parsley is to place the sprigs in a mug and snip into them with a pair of scissors.

Nuts Toasted flaked almonds and peeled and chopped pistachio nuts are both suitable garnishes.

Toasted Croûtons Instead of frying bread croûtons, make a healthier version by toasting bread and cutting it into squares immediately it is cooked, before it cools.

Vegetable Strips and Slices Finely cut carrot, leek, spinach or cabbage are all useful garnishes. Blanch them in boiling water for a few seconds and drain well.

Bacon Crisply grilled bacon, crumbled into small pieces, is an interesting and tasty topping for pale, smooth soups, especially when combined with chopped parsley or other herbs.

NUTRITION NOTE

Grilling allows the fat to drip away from bacon during cooking and it is the preferred cooking method for a healthy diet. Bacon which is grilled until really crisp gives up much of its fat during cooking. Crumble the rashers on to absorbent kitchen paper and shake them well to absorb any surface fat before setting them aside to cool.

   Instead of frying poppadoms to serve with soup (below), cook them under a hot grill. Place the grill pan well away from the heat source so that the poppadoms have plenty of room to bubble up and expand, also to avoid burning them before they are fully cooked.

TO SERVE WITH SOUP

Any type of bread goes well with soup – thin bread and butter is ideal for light soups, while chunky French bread or thick slices of wholemeal bread are ideal for hearty soups. Wedges cut from a cottage loaf or a variety of shaped bread rolls are also ideal. Here are a few alternative accompaniments to bread:

Melba Toast To make Melba toast, lightly toast both sides of medium bread slices. Working quickly, cut off the crusts, then slice each piece of toast horizontally to give two very thin pieces. Place the pieces under a hot grill, keeping them well away from the heat source to avoid burning them, and cook until browned and slightly curled. Cool on a wire rack. When cold, serve at once or store in an airtight container or tin for up to a week.

Warm Biscuits Warm Bath Oliver or water biscuits briefly in the oven to serve with soup.

Crisp Poppadoms These are a good accompaniment for spicy soups.

Pancakes Finely shred small pancakes and sprinkle them into clear soup. Alternatively, spread them with low-fat soft cheese with herbs, roll them up and slice them into pinwheels to serve separately.

Garlic Dip Instead of a garlic-flavoured mayonnaise, a traditional accompaniment for fish soups, flavour fromage frais with garlic and chopped parsley or snipped chives. Serve this with crisp toasted slices of French bread.

Blue Cheese Spread Mash a little blue cheese with sufficient fromage frais to make a soft spread. Top crackers or oatcakes with the spread, then offer them with soups such as celery or cauliflower.

Coconut Soup

This unusual soup is delicately flavoured but quite rich, with
a very smooth, creamy texture.

FOOD VALUES	TOTAL	PER PORTION
Protein	31g	8g
Carbohydrate	55g	14g
Fat	50g	13g
Fibre	5g	1g
kcals	777	194

25 g / 1 oz desiccated
   coconut or 40 g / 1 ½ oz
   shelled fresh coconut,
   grated
600 ml / 1 pint good ham
   stock, preferably from a
   smoked gammon joint
1 small onion, thinly sliced
1 bay leaf
40 g / 1 ½ oz butter
60 ml / 4 tbsp plain flour
pinch of mace
2.5 ml / ½ tsp sugar
pepper
300 ml / ½ pint reduced-fat
   single cream or fromage
   frais

Place the coconut in a saucepan with the stock. Add
the onion and bay leaf, and bring to the boil. Lower
the heat so that the stock is barely simmering, cover
the pan tightly and leave over low heat for 1 hour.
Strain into a bowl, squeezing all the liquid from the
coconut mixture.

Melt the butter in the rinsed-out pan. Stir in the
flour and gradually add the strained stock, stirring
all the time. Add a little mace, the sugar and pepper
to taste – the soup is unlikely to need salt as ham
stock is salty.

Bring to the boil, stirring, then lower the heat and
simmer for 3 minutes. Add the cream or fromage
frais, stir well and heat for a few seconds without
boiling. Serve at once.

SERVES 4

NUTRITION NOTE

Coconut has a high fat content and, unlike many other vegetable fats, is
particularly rich in saturated fats. The soup is rich and interesting as a special-
occasion starter but is not the sort of soup to serve to the family on an
everyday basis.

Chilled Avocado Soup

FOOD VALUES	TOTAL	PER PORTION
Protein	31g	5g
Carbohydrate	28g	5g
Fat	118g	20g
Fibre	20g	3g
kcals	1285	214

4 ripe avocados
juice of 1 lemon
500 ml / 17 fl oz homemade
   or canned consommé
250 ml / 8 fl oz soured
   cream or fromage frais
salt and pepper
30 ml / 2 tbsp snipped chives
   or spring onion green

Scoop the flesh from the avocados into a sieve set over a bowl. Spoon the lemon juice over the top and then rub the avocados through the sieve. Stir in the consommé and soured cream or fromage frais.

Add salt and pepper to taste, cover the bowl and refrigerate for 2-3 hours. Just before serving, stir in the chives or spring onions.

SERVES 6

NUTRITION NOTE

Delicately flavoured avocado is the basis of many delicious light dishes, but it should be remembered that the avocado is naturally rich in fat and therefore also has a high calorie content.

Vichysoisse

A simple soup which can be served hot but also
tastes good when chilled.

FOOD VALUES	TOTAL	PER PORTION (4)
Protein	31g	8g
Carbohydrate	123g	31g
Fat	59g	15g
Fibre	19g	5g
kcals	1124	281

25 g / 1 oz butter
450 g / 1 lb leeks, white parts only, trimmed, sliced and washed
2 onions, chopped
450 g / 1 lb potatoes, cubed
900 ml / 1½ pints Chicken Stock (page 20)
salt and pepper
150 ml / ¼ pint milk
150 ml / ¼ pint reduced-fat single cream or fromage frais
snipped chives to garnish

Melt the butter in a saucepan, add the leeks, onions and potatoes and fry gently for 10 minutes without browning. Stir in the stock, with salt and pepper to taste. Bring to the boil, lower the heat and simmer for about 30 minutes or until all the vegetables are soft.

Purée the mixture in a blender or food processor, or press through a sieve into a bowl. Cool quickly, then stir in the milk and cream. Add more salt and pepper if required. Cover and chill for 4-6 hours. Serve in chilled individual bowls, sprinkled with chives.

SERVES 4 TO 6

FREEZER TIP

Make the soup as above, but use only 1 onion and 600 ml / 1 pint chicken stock. After puréeing the vegetables and stock, cool the mixture quickly and freeze in a rigid container. Thaw overnight in the refrigerator. Stir in the remaining stock with the milk and cream, then chill for at least 2 hours more before serving.

MAIN COURSE SOUPS

Smoked Haddock Chowder

FOOD VALUES	TOTAL	PER PORTION (4)
Protein	156g	39g
Carbohydrate	84g	21g
Fat	58g	15g
Fibre	3g	1g
kcals	1463	366

450 g / 1 lb smoked haddock
   fillet, skinned
750 ml / 1 ¼ pints milk
25 g / 1 oz butter
1 small onion, finely
   chopped
100 g / 4 oz mushrooms,
   finely chopped
25 g / 1 oz plain flour
250 ml / 8 fl oz fromage frais
freshly ground black pepper

Put the haddock fillets into a saucepan with the milk and heat to simmering point. Simmer for about 10 minutes until just tender. Drain the fish, reserving the cooking liquid, remove the skin and shred lightly.

Melt the butter in a clean pan, add the onion and mushrooms and fry gently for about 10 minutes until soft. Do not allow the onion to colour.

Stir in the flour and cook for 1 minute, stirring constantly. Gradually add the fish-flavoured milk, stirring until smooth. Bring to the boil, lower the heat and simmer until thickened.

Off the heat, add the fromage frais and the shredded haddock. Return the pan to the heat and warm through gently. Do not allow the soup to boil after adding the fromage frais. Top with a generous grinding of black pepper and serve at once.

SERVES 4 TO 6

MRS BEETON'S TIP

Reserve a few perfect mushrooms for a garnish if liked. Slice them thinly and sprinkle a few slices on top of each portion of soup. It is not necessary to cook the mushrooms.

Mussel Soup

FOOD VALUES	TOTAL	PER PORTION (4)
Protein	50g	13g
Carbohydrate	4g	1g
Fat	43g	11g
Fibre	—	—
kcals	676	169

800 g / 1¾ lb mussels
125 ml / 4 fl oz white wine
20 ml / 4 tsp lemon juice
750 ml / 1¼ pints Fish
    Stock (page 21)
25 g / 1 oz butter
30 ml / 2 tbsp plain flour
salt and pepper
20 ml / 4 tsp chopped
    parsley
1 egg yolk
75 ml / 5 tbsp reduced-fat
    single cream

Wash, scrape and beard the mussels following the instructions in Mrs Beeton's Tip. Put them in a large saucepan with the wine and lemon juice. Add 250 ml / 8 fl oz of the fish stock, cover the pan tightly and simmer for 8-10 minutes or until the mussels have opened. Discard any that remain shut.

Strain the cooking liquid through muslin or a very fine sieve into a jug containing the remaining fish stock. Shell the mussels.

Melt the butter in a deep saucepan. Stir in the flour and cook gently for 1 minute. Gradually add the fish stock, stirring constantly. Bring to the boil and cook for 2 minutes, still stirring. Add salt and pepper to taste and stir in the chopped parsley.

In a small bowl, mix the egg yolk with the cream. Stir a little of the hot soup into the egg mixture, mix well, then add the contents of the bowl to the soup, stirring the soup over low heat until it thickens. Add the mussels and reheat gently, without boiling. Serve at once.

SERVES 4 TO 6

MRS BEETON'S TIP

Scrub the mussels thoroughly and scrape off any barnacles. Discard any open shells which do not close when tapped. Pull away the dark hairy 'beard' which protrudes slightly from the shell.

Borsch

FOOD VALUES	TOTAL	PER PORTION
Protein	30g	5g
Carbohydrate	138g	23g
Fat	65g	11g
Fibre	34g	6g
kcals	1221	204

30 ml / 2 tbsp oil
1 onion, roughly chopped
1 garlic clove, sliced
1 carrot, sliced
1 turnip, sliced
1 swede, sliced
2 tomatoes, peeled and
  chopped
350 g / 12 oz raw beetroot,
  grated
1 bay leaf
2 litres / 3½ pints Rich
  Strong Stock (page 19)
30 ml / 2 tbsp tomato purée
salt and pepper
225 g / 8 oz cabbage, sliced
225 g / 8 oz potatoes, cubed
5 ml / 1 tsp cider vinegar
150 ml / ¼ pint soured
  cream or plain yogurt
chopped dill to garnish

Heat the oil in a large saucepan. Add the onion, garlic, carrot, turnip and swede and cook for 10 minutes, stirring frequently to prevent the vegetables from sticking to the base of the pan. Stir in the tomatoes and beetroot, with the bay leaf. Add the stock and tomato purée, with salt and pepper to taste. Bring to the boil, lower the heat, cover and simmer for 1 hour.

Add the sliced cabbage and cubed potato. Stir in the vinegar and simmer for 15 minutes more or until the potato cubes are tender. Taste the soup and add more salt and pepper, if required.

Leave to stand for 5 minutes. Serve topped with soured cream or plain yogurt and garnished with chopped dill.

SERVES 6

NUTRITION NOTE

The values given apply to borsch served with soured cream. If low-fat yogurt is used instead, the total fat content is reduced to 36 g and the total kilocalories are 1,003.

Cabbage Soup

Cabbage and bacon go wonderfully well together, a fact that is celebrated in this hearty soup.

FOOD VALUES	TOTAL	PER PORTION
Protein	44g	6g
Carbohydrate	52g	7g
Fat	91g	11g
Fibre	26g	3g
· kcals	1195	149

15 ml / 1 tbsp oil
175 g / 6 oz rindless bacon rashers, chopped
2 carrots, thinly sliced
1 large onion, thinly sliced
1 large cabbage, shredded
1.1 litres / 2 pints White Stock (page 18)
pepper to taste
toasted croûtons (page 30) to serve (optional)

Heat the oil in a large heavy-bottomed saucepan or flameproof casserole. Add the bacon and cook, stirring, for 5 minutes. Add the carrots and onion, then cook gently for 10 minutes. Stir in the cabbage and add the stock. Bring to the boil, lower the heat and cover the pan. Simmer for 45 minutes, until the vegetables are tender and the soup well flavoured.

Taste the soup for seasoning and add pepper. The bacon usually makes the soup sufficiently salty, depending on the stock. Skim off any excess surface fat, then serve the soup very hot, with croûtons, if liked.

SERVES 8

MRS BEETON'S TIP

If the soup is slightly too salty when cooked, add 2 peeled and diced potatoes, and simmer for 20-30 minutes, keeping the pan closely covered.

MAKING A MEAL OF SOUP

Soup can make a practical, economical and nutritious family meal. With the right combination of ingredients and served in generous portions a good soup will more than satisfy hungry appetites. Main meal soups may derive their protein content from fish, poultry, meat or pulses. However, good mixed vegetable soups are particularly economical and satisfying and can be served with bread and cheese to make well-balanced meals.

INGREDIENTS FOR SATISFYING SOUPS

Mixed Vegetables Chunks of potato; sliced carrot; diced swede, turnip or parsnip; florets of broccoli or cauliflower; shredded green, white or red cabbage; sliced courgettes; cut French beans; broad beans or peas are all ideal ingredients for a mixed vegetable soup. Sliced celery, onion, a bay leaf, parsley stalks and thyme sprigs are essential for a good flavour. For best results, simmer the stock and flavouring ingredients for 20 minutes before adding the other vegetables, then add the root vegetables first as they take longer to cook. Ingredients which need little cooking, such as sliced courgettes, canned sweetcorn or frozen peas or beans, should be added towards the end of cooking. Simmer the soup. Leave the soup chunky.

Rice and Other Grains Rice adds body and bite to flavoursome fish, poultry and meat stocks without detracting from the flavour of the main ingredient.

Pearl barley is a traditional thickening ingredient for soup; it is usually added in small quantities and boiled for long periods until the grain virtually disintegrates and the soup thickens. However, it may also be added in the same proportions as rice and cooked for about 20 minutes, preserving the texture of the barley in much the same way as for rice.

Roasted buckwheat may be added in small quantities to thicken a soup as it quickly disintegrates when boiled with flavoursome stock and vegetables.

Pasta Pasta especially manufactured for adding to soup (tiny shells, wheels and other small shapes) cooks extremely quickly, so soup pasta should be added about 5 minutes before serving the soup. If the soup is left to stand for any length of time the pasta swells, absorbing the stock so that the soup resembles an overcooked pasta dish.

Ordinary pasta can be added to soup. The soup should be thin or there must be plenty of stock in which to cook the pasta. Shapes or elbow macaroni are suitable; long spaghetti or macaroni can be broken into short lengths before they are added to the soup.

Beans and Pulses Dried beans should be boiled separately in water for 10 minutes, then added to plenty of thin soup and simmered until cooked. Canned beans can be added towards the end of the cooking time.

Red lentils and split peas are classic ingredients for turning ham stock into a hearty soup. They are boiled until they disintegrate into the stock to thicken and flavour it. The pulses balance the saltiness of the meat stock. Red lentils

are excellent for making thickened soups, while green and brown lentils are also nutritious ingredients which add bite to a soup as they stay whole.

Bread Bread makes a surprisingly good thickener for soup as it absorbs liquid during cooking and becomes completely incorporated with the soup. Sliced bread may also be added to soup – thickly slice day-old French bread, place it the bottom of a tureen, then pour boiling-hot soup over it. Allow to stand, covered, for 10-15 minutes before serving. Toasted bread may be floated in soup before serving or slices of bread may be grilled or baked on top of the soup in its serving dishes – French onion soup, topped with bread and cheese, is the classic example of this method.

THICKENING SOUPS

Chunky soups do not necessarily need any additional thickening as the thin soup is complemented by chunks of vegetables or other ingredients. For a soup which is both thickened and chunky, purée a small portion of the soup, then return it to the main pot of soup – this way, the liquid is thickened but the soup will retain plenty of pieces of vegetables.

Roux A roux mixture of fat and flour may be used to thicken some soups, but this depends on the ingredients. Onion soup may be prepared by this method if the onions are first cooked for a long period in a little fat until they are thoroughly tender. Then the flour may be stirred in and the stock added. This method avoids the soup having to be simmered for a long time which can cause the flour thickening to burn slightly on the bottom of the pan if the soup is not stirred regularly and the heat controlled. The other main disadvantage of a roux is that a significant amount of butter or other fat must be used in the initial cooking to make the flour paste.

Beurre Manié Another classic thickening, this consists of a butter and flour paste which is added to the soup in lumps and whisked in. The soup is then simmered for a few minutes before serving. As with a roux, the butter or fat used to make the paste increases the fat content of the soup.

Potatoes and Vegetables Potatoes provide one of the best forms of thickening for soup as they give an excellent texture. Carrots and other root vegetables also thicken soups well; celery and the lighter-textured vegetables make a slightly thinner purée; when making a soup using these vegetables add a small potato to give the required consistency when the mixture is puréed.

Beans and Pulses These excellent thickeners do not require the addition of fat and they increase the food value of a main meal soup.

Rice, Grains and Pasta Ideal for main meal soups, these ingredients lightly thicken the liquid and make soups substantial and satisfying.

Egg Yolks and Cream or Fromage Frais Egg yolks beaten with cream or fromage frais and a little of the hot soup may be stirred in just before the soup is served and warmed gently if necessary. This mixture thickens fine or puréed soups very slightly, at the same time enriching the soup. Obviously, these ingredients increase the fat content of the soup. Cream should not be added to everyday soups but reserved for special occasions.

Cock-a-leekie

FOOD VALUES	TOTAL	PER PORTION (6)
Protein	180g	30g
Carbohydrate	47g	8g
Fat	73g	12g
Fibre	16g	3g
kcals	1560	260

100 g / 4 oz prunes
450 g / 1 lb leeks, trimmed,
    sliced and washed
1 (1.4 kg / 3 lb) chicken
3 rindless bacon rashers,
    chopped
2.5 ml / ½ tsp salt
1 bouquet garni
1.25 ml / ¼ tsp pepper

Soak the prunes overnight in a small bowl of water, then drain them and remove the stones. Set aside, with about one-third of the drained leek slices.

Put the chicken, with its giblets if available, and bacon in a deep saucepan. Add cold water to cover (about 2 litres / 3½ pints). Stir in the salt and bring slowly to simmering point.

Add the remaining leeks to the pan, with the bouquet garni and pepper. Cover, then simmer gently for about 3 hours or until the chicken is cooked through and tender.

Carefully remove the chicken, discard the skin, then carve off the meat and cut it into fairly large serving pieces. Discard the giblets. Return the chicken meat to the soup and add the reserved prunes and leeks. Simmer gently for about 30 minutes, until the prunes are cooked but not broken. Skim off the surface fat and check seasoning before serving.

SERVES 6 TO 8

MRS BEETON'S TIP

Ready-to-eat dried prunes may be used. There is no need to presoak them.

Scotch Broth

This economical soup was originally intended to furnish two meals: the meat was removed after cooking and served separately. Today it is more usual to cut up the meat and add it to the soup.

FOOD VALUES	TOTAL	PER PORTION
Protein	140g	35g
Carbohydrate	82g	21g
Fat	75g	19g
Fibre	22g	6g
kcals	1542	386

25 g / 1 oz pearl barley
450 g / 1 lb middle neck of lamb, trimmed of excess fat
1.4 litres / 2½ pints White Stock (page 18) or Chicken Stock (page 20)
1 onion, chopped
1 leek, trimmed, sliced and washed
2 carrots, sliced
1 swede, cubed
salt and pepper

Put the barley in a small saucepan with water to cover. Bring to the boil, then drain off the water and transfer the barley to a large pan with the meat and stock. Bring the mixture to the boil, skim off any scum on the surface, then lower the heat and simmer gently for 2 hours.

Add the vegetables with plenty of salt and pepper. Simmer for a further 45-60 minutes. Lift out the meat, remove it from the bones, and roughly chop it. Skim off any fat from the broth, add more salt and pepper if required, then replace the chopped meat. Serve very hot.

SERVES 4

PRESSURE COOKER TIP

It is not necessary to blanch the barley. Simply combine the ingredients in the cooker, reducing the amount of stock to 900 ml / 1½ pints. The cooker should not be more than half full. Put the lid on, bring to 15 lb pressure and cook for 10 minutes. Reduce the pressure slowly. Continue as above, reheating the soup in the open pan, and adding more stock if liked.

Bean Soup

FOOD VALUES	TOTAL	PER PORTION (6)
Protein	114g	19g
Carbohydrate	223g	37g
Fat	47g	8g
Fibre	3g	1g
kcals	1715	286

450 g / 1 lb haricot beans,
  soaked overnight in water
  to cover
100 g / 4 oz fat bacon, diced
2 onions, sliced
10 ml / 2 tsp dried thyme
salt and pepper
15 ml / 1 tbsp chopped
  parsley

Drain the soaked beans. Put them in a large heavy-bottomed saucepan. Add 2.25 litres / 4 pints water and bring to the boil. Boil vigorously for 10 minutes, then lower the heat and simmer for 45 minutes or until almost tender. Drain, reserving the stock.

Put the bacon in the clean pan and heat gently until the fat runs. Add the onions and fry over moderate heat for 3-4 minutes. Stir in the beans with the thyme. Add the reserved bean stock, with salt and pepper to taste. Simmer for 1 hour, stirring occasionally to prevent the soup from sticking. Check the seasoning and add more salt and pepper if required. Stir in the parsley and serve at once.

SERVES 6 TO 8

VARIATIONS

Two-bean Soup Use half red kidney beans instead of haricot beans alone. Add 1 diced green pepper with the onions.
Vegetarian Bean Soup Omit the bacon and fry the onions in 25 g / 1 oz butter with 1 crushed garlic clove. Stir in 45 ml / 3 tbsp tahini with the parsley.

Soup à la Crecy

FOOD VALUES	TOTAL	PER PORTION
Protein	46g	8g
Carbohydrate	212g	35g
Fat	24g	4g
Fibre	25g	4g
kcals	1200	200

100 g / 4 oz long-grain
  brown rice
15 ml / 1 tbsp oil
4 carrots, sliced
2 onions, thinly sliced
100 g / 4 oz red lentils
1.75 litres / 3 pints Chicken
  Stock (page 20)
1 lettuce, shredded
50 g / 2 oz fresh wholemeal
  breadcrumbs
salt and pepper

Place the rice in a saucepan and add plenty of water, then bring to the boil. Reduce the heat so that the water simmers, cover the pan and cook for 25 minutes, or until the rice is just tender. Drain thoroughly, rinse under cold water and drain again. Set aside.

Heat the oil in a large saucepan, add the carrots and onions and fry over gentle heat for about 10 minutes until soft. Stir in the lentils, then add the stock. Bring to the boil, lower the heat and simmer for 20 minutes, stirring occasionally.

Stir in the lettuce and breadcrumbs, with plenty of salt and pepper. Simmer for 10 minutes more. Purée the soup in a blender or food processor, or rub through a sieve into a clean pan. Alternatively, leave the soup chunky. Add the rice and bring to the boil, stirring, then simmer for 2 minutes and serve.

SERVES 6

NUTRITION NOTE

Beans and pulses (in the soup on the left) are an excellent source of protein. In a vegetarian diet they play an important role in making up for protein which might otherwise be obtained from animal sources. Soya beans are a particularly good source, providing protein equivalent in value to that provided by animal sources.

Gazpacho

FOOD VALUES	TOTAL	PER PORTION
Protein	20g	5g
Carbohydrate	93g	23g
Fat	78g	20g
Fibre	14g	4g
kcals	1129	282

2 thick slices of bread, cubed
1 litre / 1¾ pints tomato juice
1 small onion, finely chopped
2 garlic cloves, crushed
½ cucumber, finely chopped
1 green pepper, seeded and chopped
6 tomatoes, peeled and chopped
75 ml / 3 fl oz olive oil
30 ml / 2 tbsp red wine vinegar
1.25 ml / ¼ tsp dried oregano
1.25 ml / ¼ tsp dried mixed herbs
salt and pepper

TO SERVE
toasted croûtons (page 30)
diced cucumber
diced onion
black olives

Put the bread cubes in a large bowl with the tomato juice. Leave to soak for 5 minutes, then add the chopped vegetables. Stir in the olive oil, cover and leave to stand for 1 hour.

Purée the soup in a blender or food processor, then rub through a sieve into a clean bowl. Stir in the vinegar and herbs, with salt and pepper to taste. Cover the bowl closely and chill for 2-3 hours. Serve with the suggested accompaniments, in separate bowls.

SERVES 4

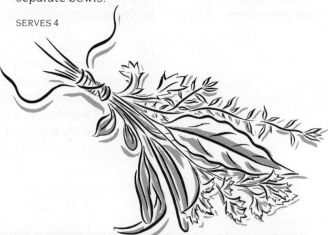

MRS BEETON'S TIP

If you do not have a blender, strain the mixture, reserving the tomato juice, then pound the vegetables and bread to a paste in a mortar with a pestle; rub through a sieve into a clean bowl. Return the tomato juice to the bowl and add the vinegar, herbs and seasoning. Chill as suggested above.

SALADS AND COLD STARTERS

Grapefruit and Chicory Salad

FOOD VALUES	TOTAL	PER PORTION
Protein	5g	1g
Carbohydrate	37g	6g
Fat	47g	8g
Fibre	8g	1g
kcals	568	95

3 grapefruit
3 small heads of chicory
50 g / 2 oz seedless raisins
15 ml / 1 tbsp grapefruit
*   juice*
45 ml / 3 tbsp oil
2.5 ml / ½ tsp French
*   mustard*
salt and pepper
mustard and cress to
*   garnish*

Cut the grapefruit in half. Cut the fruit into segments and put them into a bowl. Remove all the pulp and pith from the grapefruit shells; stand the shells upside down on absorbent kitchen paper to drain.

Shred the chicory, reserving some neat rounds for the garnish, and add to the grapefruit segments with all the remaining ingredients except the garnish. Toss the mixture lightly together, then pile back into the grapefruit shells. Garnish with the mustard and cress and reserved chicory and serve at once.

SERVES 6

Avocado and Tomato Cocktails

FOOD VALUES	TOTAL	PER PORTION
Protein	19g	5g
Carbohydrate	27g	7g
Fat	60g	15g
Fibre	12g	3g
kcals	720	180

2 ripe avocados
2 ripe tomatoes, peeled and
    diced

DRESSING
5 ml / 1 tsp caster sugar
2.5 ml / ½ tsp dry mustard
salt and paprika
150 ml / ¼ pint fromage
    frais
15 ml / 1 tbsp snipped chives

Cut the avocados in half lengthways; remove the stones. Keeping the skins intact, scoop out and dice or roughly chop the flesh. Mix with the tomatoes, then spoon the mixture back into the shells or into individual dishes.

To make the dressing, mix the sugar, mustard, salt and a pinch of paprika. Gradually stir in the fromage frais until smooth. Stir in the chives. Top the avocados with the dressing and serve.

SERVES 4

Orange and Ortanique Salad

FOOD VALUES	TOTAL	PER PORTION
Protein	14g	2g
Carbohydrate	106g	18g
Fat	82g	14g
Fibre	20g	3g
kcals	1187	198

3 oranges, peeled and sliced

3 ortaniques, peeled and sliced (see Mrs Beeton's Tip)

1 mild Italian or Spanish onion, cut in rings

12 black olives

30 ml / 2 tbsp chopped mint to garnish

DRESSING

75 ml / 5 tbsp olive oil

30 ml / 2 tbsp orange juice

15 ml / 1 tbsp red wine vinegar

5 ml / 1 tsp soy sauce

5 ml / 1 tsp liquid honey

salt and pepper

Make the dressing by mixing all the ingredients in a screw-topped jar. Close the jar tightly and shake vigorously until well blended.

Put the dressing in a large bowl and add the orange, ortanique and onion slices. Cover the bowl and set aside for 1-2 hours.

When ready to serve, arrange the drained fruit and onion slices on a large platter, add the olives and drizzle the remaining dressing over the top. Sprinkle with the mint.

SERVES 6

MRS BEETON'S TIP

The ortanique – a cross between an orange and a tangerine – was developed in Jamaica. The fruit is easy to peel and segment, and is very sweet and juicy. If unavailable, substitute tangerines, grapefruit or limes.

Caesar Salad

As the egg in this salad is only lightly cooked, it is very important that it be perfectly fresh, and purchased from a reputable source.

FOOD VALUES	TOTAL	PER PORTION
Protein	63g	11g
Carbohydrate	104g	17g
Fat	191g	32g
Fibre	12g	2g
kcals	2357	393

3 garlic cloves, peeled but left whole
2 cos lettuces, separated into leaves
150 ml / ¼ pint olive oil
4 large thick slices of bread, crusts removed and cubed
1 egg
juice of 1 lemon
1 (50 g / 2 oz) can anchovy fillets, drained
50 g / 2 oz Parmesan cheese, grated
salt and pepper

Cut 1 garlic clove in half and rub it all around a salad bowl. Wash the lettuce leaves and dry them thoroughly. Tear into small pieces and put in the salad bowl.

Heat 60 ml / 4 tbsp of the olive oil in a small frying pan, add the remaining garlic cloves and fry over gentle heat for 1 minute. Add the bread cubes and fry until golden on all sides. Remove from the pan with a slotted spoon and drain on absorbent kitchen paper. Discard the garlic and oil in the pan.

Add the remaining olive oil to the lettuce and toss until every leaf is coated. Bring a small saucepan of water to the boil, add the egg and cook for 1 minute. Using a slotted spoon remove it from the water and break it over the lettuce. Add the lemon juice, anchovies, cheese, salt and pepper and toss lightly.

Add the croûtons of fried bread and toss again. Serve while the croûtons are still crisp.

SERVES 6

NUTRITION NOTE

As a general rule, the stronger the flavour of a hard cheese, or the more mature it is, then the higher the fat content.

FIBRE IN THE DIET

Dietary fibre is carbohydrate in the form of cellulose or similar substances which the body cannot digest but which plays a vital role in the removal of waste products from the body. There are various forms of fibre, derived from fruit and vegetables as well as from cereals and grains, and they should all be included in the diet. Just as it is sensible to balance the intake of nutrients and avoid putting too much emphasis on any one food, it is possible to adopt an excessive approach to fibre and to try to add unnaturally large amounts at every opportunity. If you ensure that your diet includes a good range of foods which contain different forms of fibre, there should be no need to supplement this by eating excessive quantities of bran and other high-fibre products.

Bread and Flour Products

Wholemeal bread is a good source of dietary fibre because it can be enjoyed in significant and regular quantities. Wholemeal bread may be eaten for breakfast as well as for lunch or supper as an accompaniment to a simple dish or to make sandwiches. Buying an uncut loaf and cutting thick slices is a good idea when making sandwiches every day.

Other vehicles for wholemeal flour include pasta and the products of home-baking, such as pastry. Using half and half white and wholemeal flour for making pastry when preparing everyday meals improves the fibre content of the meal considerably. Pies, quiches or Cornish pasties can all be made from this type of pastry.

Cereals and Grains

Breakfast cereals probably make the most significant contribution in terms of fibre in the diet of many people. If you do eat cereal regularly for breakfast, it is a good idea to buy some types which have a high fibre content.

Oats, rice and other grains also make a contribution to fibre in the diet. Uncooked oats are thought to be particularly valuable as a source of soluble fibre, so muesli is useful in a balanced diet. Although refined grains and cereals need not be avoided it is a good idea to include some whole grains, such as brown rice.

Beans and Pulses

These have a high fibre content and many types are a rich source of vegetable protein.

Fruit and Vegetables

The role of these foods is enormously important in balancing the energy intake of the diet and their contribution to the overall fibre content of the diet is substantial. Raw fruit and vegetables in salads are especially valuable for the vitamins they can offer as well as for the fibre content. It is a good idea always to eat the peel on fruit and vegetables, such as baked potatoes.

HIGH FIBRE FOODS

A checklist of some of the everyday foods which provide a useful supply of fibre:

- Beans – baked beans, canned or dried beans (such as red kidney and haricot), runner beans
- Biscuits with a high fibre content – but avoid eating too many of the varieties which have a high sugar content
- Breakfast Cereals – wholewheat cereals and bran cereals, muesli and porridge oats
- Grains such as wheat, cracked wheat, bulgur, buckwheat, pot barley and brown rice
- Flour, especially wholemeal flour, and flour products
- Fruit – raw fresh fruit, especially apples (with their peel) and dried fruits, such as prunes and figs
- Vegetables – carrots, cabbage, spinach, potatoes, peas, celery and so on
- Wholefoods – these are foods which are not highly refined, usually thought of as cereal and grain products

BREAKFAST: AN OPPORTUNITY TO TOP UP ON FIBRE

The traditional view of breakfast being the most important meal of the day for providing fuel for the day ahead still holds true and it also provides an excellent opportunity for including cereal-based fibre in the diet.

Cereals and wholemeal toast or bread are both ideal foods for breakfast not only for their satisfying characteristics but also for the fibre they provide. It is worth mentioning that the sugar and fat content of breakfast should be monitored. Some breakfast cereals have a high sugar content, particularly those manufactured to appeal to children.

It may be sensible for adults who eat cereal everyday for breakfast to use semi-skimmed milk, to lower the fat content of the meal – but this does depend on the average fat content of meals eaten over the rest of the day. Similarly, a couple of slices of wholemeal toast which are soaked with butter are not a healthy option for everyday breakfasts.

Using wholemeal bread for sandwiches and eating plenty of fruit and vegetables with every meal are other key ways of eating an adequate supply of fibre. It is also worth remembering that a bowl of breakfast cereal with skimmed or semi-skimmed milk makes a good in-between meal snack.

Moulded Salmon Salad

FOOD VALUES	TOTAL	PER PORTION (6)
Protein	69g	12g
Carbohydrate	9g	2g
Fat	30g	5g
Fibre	3g	1g
kcals	580	97

500 ml / 17 fl oz White
   Wine Fish Stock (page
   21)
25 g / 1 oz gelatine
salt and pepper
½ unpeeled cucumber,
   sliced
2 firm tomatoes, sliced
225 g / 8 oz cooked salmon
   or 1 (397 g / 14 oz) can
   salmon, drained and
   flaked; any skin and bone
   removed

Heat the stock in a saucepan, stir in the gelatine and stir briskly until completely dissolved. Add salt and pepper to taste. Set aside to cool but do not allow to set.

Cover the bottom of a 600 ml / 1 pint mould with some cool fish stock. Chill until set. Arrange a few cucumber and tomato slices on the jelly-lined mould, then pour a little more stock over the top to keep the garnish in place. Chill again until set. Add a layer of salmon and another layer of stock, and chill again until set.

Repeat these layers until the mould is full, then cover closely and chill until required. Invert the mould on to a wetted plate (see Mrs Beeton's Tip, page 61) to serve.

SERVES 4 TO 6

NUTRITION NOTE

This salad is ideal for a low-fat lunch. Serve it with baked potatoes, each topped with a little fromage frais mixed with snipped chives. Add a tomato salad and a good mixed green salad to keep the menu light.

Camargue Mussels

FOOD VALUES	TOTAL	PER PORTION
Protein	107g	23g
Carbohydrate	1g	–
Fat	118g	15g
Fibre	–	–
kcals	1488	186

2 kg / 4½ lb mussels
1 onion, sliced
2 garlic cloves, cut in slivers
1 carrot, sliced
1 celery stick, sliced
1 bouquet garni
125 ml / 4 fl oz white wine
chopped parsley to garnish

MAYONNAISE
1 egg yolk
5 ml / 1 tsp French mustard
5 ml / 1 tsp white wine
   vinegar
salt and cayenne pepper
100 ml / 3½ fl oz sunflower
   oil
20 ml / 4 tsp lemon juice

Wash, scrape and beard the mussels (see Mrs Beeton's Tip, page 37). Put them in a large saucepan. Tuck the sliced vegetables among the mussels and add the bouquet garni. Pour over the wine and add 125 ml / 4 fl oz water. Place the pan over moderate heat and bring to the boil. As soon as the liquid bubbles up over the mussels, shake the pan several times, cover, lower the heat and simmer until the mussels have opened. Discard any that remain shut. With a slotted spoon remove the mussels from the stock. Arrange them, on their half shells, on a large flat dish. Strain the cooking liquid into a jug and cool.

Make the mayonnaise. Blend the egg yolk, mustard and vinegar with salt and cayenne to taste, in a bowl. Using a balloon whisk, beat in the oil very gradually, drop by drop. When about half the oil has been dripped in add the rest of the oil in a slow thin stream. Stir in the lemon juice and cooking liquid. Spoon the mayonnaise over the mussels and sprinkle with parsley. Serve chilled.

SERVES 8

NUTRITION NOTE

For a less-rich dressing, use half mayonnaise and half fromage frais or plain yogurt. For a low-fat dressing, season fromage frais to taste, then stir in a little mustard and add some finely chopped parsley or snipped chives.

Marinated Herring

FOOD VALUES	TOTAL	PER PORTION
Protein	89g	15g
Carbohydrate	24g	4g
Fat	93g	16g
Fibre	4g	1g
kcals	1282	214

3 salted herrings, cleaned

MARINADE
2 onions, chopped
1-2 bay leaves
30 ml / 2 tbsp caster sugar
60 ml / 4 tbsp distilled
  vinegar (see Mrs Beeton's
  Tip)
45 ml / 3 tbsp tomato purée

Pat the herrings dry with absorbent kitchen paper. Lay them in a shallow glass or enamel bowl. Pour over cold water to cover, then cover the bowl tightly. Set aside for 6 hours in a cold place.

Make the marinade by combining all the ingredients in a large shallow dish. Add 15 ml / 1 tbsp water and mix well.

Drain the herrings and pat dry with absorbent kitchen paper. Cut them into small pieces, discarding the bones. Add the herring pieces to the marinade and mix well. Cover the dish and marinate for 48 hours, stirring several times.

SERVES 6

MRS BEETON'S TIP

Vinegars vary considerably in the percentage of acetic acid they contain. Malt and cider vinegars are milder than wine vinegars. The strongest vinegars are labelled fortified or distilled. Distilled vinegar is usually made from malt. It is colourless. If you find it difficult to obtain, use pickling vinegar instead.

Herring Rolls

FOOD VALUES	TOTAL	PER PORTION
Protein	129g	32g
Carbohydrate	–	–
Fat	154g	39g
Fibre	–	–
kcals	1905	476

25 g / 1 oz butter, softened
2 hard-boiled eggs, yolks
 and whites separated and
 finely chopped
8 anchovy fillets, finely
 chopped
cayenne pepper
4 rollmop herrings, each
 divided into 2 fillets
lemon juice

GARNISH
8 lemon slices
4-6 sliced gherkins
1 small diced beetroot
chopped parsley

Cream the butter in a bowl with the hard-boiled egg yolks and anchovies. Add a pinch of cayenne and mix well.

Spread most of the butter mixture on the rollmops and roll up firmly. Spread the remaining mixture thinly on the round ends of each roll and dip in the chopped egg white. Sprinkle the rolls with lemon juice and arrange on a plate, garnished with lemon slices, gherkins, beetroot and parsley.

SERVES 4

VARIATION

Salted Herring Rolls Use salted herrings instead of rollmops. Soak them in cold water for several hours before use, then fillet, being careful to remove all the bones.

Soused Herrings

Soused herrings make an excellent starter or light summer meal.
Small mackerel or mackerel fillets can be soused in the same way.
Both are excellent served with a dish of soured cream flavoured
with plenty of chopped fresh dill.

FOOD VALUES	TOTAL	PER PORTION
Protein	176g	29g
Carbohydrate	–	–
Fat	194g	32g
Fibre	–	–
kcals	2457	410

6 herrings, scaled, heads and
    tails removed, and boned
salt and pepper
150 ml / ¼ pint malt
    vinegar
15 ml / 1 tbsp pickling spice
4 bay leaves
2 small onions, sliced in
    rings

Set the oven at 150°C / 300°F / gas 2. Season the
herrings with salt and pepper. Roll up the fillets,
skin side in, from the tail end. Place neatly and fairly
close together in an ovenproof baking dish.

In a jug, mix the vinegar with 100 ml / 3½ fl oz water.
Pour over the herrings, sprinkle with pickling spice
and add the bay leaves. Lay the onion rings on top.
Cover the dish loosely with foil and bake for 1½
hours. Remove from the oven and leave to cool
completely. Use a slotted spoon to lift the rolls
from the cooking liquor when serving.

SERVES 6

NUTRITION NOTE

Oily fish, such as herring or mackerel, are rich in fat-soluble vitamins A and D.

Prawn Cocktail

Perennially popular Prawn Cocktail also makes a good
light lunch or supper dish.

FOOD VALUES	TOTAL	PER PORTION
Protein	58g	15g
Carbohydrate	9g	2g
Fat	5g	1g
Fibre	1g	–
kcals	308	77

4 *lettuce leaves, shredded*
225 *g / 8 oz peeled cooked
prawns*
75 *ml / 5 tbsp fromage frais*
15 *ml / 1 tbsp tomato purée*
few drops of Tabasco sauce
5 *ml / 1 tsp chilli vinegar or
tarragon vinegar
(optional)*
salt and pepper
4 *whole cooked prawns to
garnish*

Place a little shredded lettuce on the base of 4 glass
dishes. Put the prawns on top. Mix the fromage frais
with the tomato purée and add a few drops of
Tabasco sauce. Stir in the vinegar, if liked, with salt
and pepper to taste. Spoon the mayonnaise mixture
over the prawns and garnish each dish with a whole
cooked prawn, preferably in the shell. Serve with
brown bread and butter, if liked.

SERVES 4

VARIATIONS

Avocado Ritz Serve the prawns and dressing on
avocado halves. Cut the avocados in half and
remove the stones just before topping and serving.
If there is likely to be any delay, brush the avocado
flesh with lemon juice to prevent discoloration.
Prawn and Horseradish Cocktail Omit the
Tabasco sauce and vinegar from the recipe above
and add 5 ml / 1 tsp grated fresh horseradish or
15 ml / 1 tbsp creamed horseradish.

NUTRITION NOTE

Prawns, lobster and crab meat are all ideal for low-fat first courses; however
any benefit is lost when cream and other rich dressings are added. Fromage
frais is a good compromise as it can be virtually fat free, yet does not have the
sharp tang associated with low-fat plain yogurt. Even fromage frais with an
8 per cent fat content is a significant improvement on mayonnaise or cream.

Fresh Salmon Mousse

FOOD VALUES	TOTAL	PER PORTION (6)
Protein	112g	19g
Carbohydrate	42g	7g
Fat	90g	15g
Fibre	1g	—
kcals	1434	239

oil for greasing
450 g / 1 lb salmon fillet or
    steak (a tail piece may be
    used)
1 litre / 1¾ pints Fish Stock
    (page 21)
15 g / ½ oz gelatine
45 ml / 3 tbsp fromage frais
15 ml / 1 tbsp medium-dry
    sherry
cucumber and radish slices
    to serve

BECHAMEL SAUCE
½ small onion
½ small carrot
1 small celery stick
300 ml / ½ pint milk
1 bay leaf
few parsley stalks
1 fresh thyme sprig
1 clove
5 white peppercorns
1 blade of mace
salt
25 g / 1 oz butter
25 g / 1 oz plain flour

Brush a glass or metal fish mould with oil. Leave upside down to drain. Make the sauce. Combine the onion, carrot, celery and milk in a saucepan. Add the herbs and spices, with salt to taste. Heat to simmering point, cover, turn off the heat and allow to stand for 30 minutes to infuse. Strain into a measuring jug.

Melt the butter in a saucepan. Stir in the flour and cook over a low heat for 2-3 minutes, without allowing the mixture to colour. Gradually add the flavoured milk, stirring constantly until the mixture boils and thickens. Remove the pan from the heat, cover the surface of the sauce with damp greaseproof paper and set aside until required.

Put the salmon in a large saucepan and cover with fish stock. Bring to the boil, lower the heat and simmer for 15 minutes. Drain, cool and remove the skin and bones. Pound to a paste in a mortar or process in a blender or food processor until smooth.

Place 30 ml / 2 tbsp water in a small bowl and sprinkle the gelatine on to the liquid. Set aside for 15 minutes until the gelatine is spongy. Stand the bowl over a pan of hot water and stir the gelatine until it has dissolved completely.

Tip the salmon into a large bowl and add the cold Béchamel sauce. Mix until thoroughly blended, then add the fromage frais, sherry and dissolved gelatine. Mix well, then spoon into the prepared mould. Smooth the top, cover closely and chill for 2-3 hours until set. Turn out (see Mrs Beeton's Tip), garnish with cucumber and radish slices and serve.

SERVES 6 TO 8

VARIATION

Canned salmon may be used instead of fresh fish. Use one 213 g / 7 oz can. Drain the can liquid and use instead of water to sponge the gelatine.

MRS BEETON'S TIP

Rinse the serving platter in cold water, draining off the excess. Run the point of a sharp knife around the edge of the salmon mousse to loosen it, then dip the mould in warm water. Invert the plate on top of the mould, then, holding mould and plate firmly, turn both right side up again. The mould should lift off easily. If necessary, move the mousse to the desired position on the platter – the skin of water remaining on the plate will make this possible. Repeat the process if the mousse does not come out first time, but avoid leaving it in the warm water for too long or the design on the mousse will be blurred.

Gravad Lax

Always use fresh dill to make this marvellous
summer starter or light snack.

FOOD VALUES	TOTAL	PER PORTION (4)
Protein	186g	47g
Carbohydrate	13g	3g
Fat	182g	46g
Fibre	—	—
kcals	2441	610

2 *pieces unskinned salmon*
fillet, total weight about
1 kg / 2¼ lb, scaled
200 *g / 7 oz salt*
90 *g / 3½ oz caster sugar*
50 *g / 2 oz white*
peppercorns, crushed
90 *g / 3½ oz fresh dill, plus*
extra to garnish

MUSTARD SAUCE
30 *ml / 2 tbsp Swedish*
mustard (or other mild
mustard)
10 *ml / 2 tsp caster sugar*
15 *ml / 1 tbsp chopped fresh*
dill
45-60 *ml / 3-4 tbsp*
sunflower oil
lemon juice to taste
salt and pepper

Score the skin on each salmon fillet in 4 places. Mix the salt, sugar and peppercorns in a bowl.

Sprinkle a third of the salt mixture on the base of a shallow dish. Place one salmon fillet, skin side down, on the mixture. Cover with a further third of the salt mixture and add half the dill. Arrange the second fillet, skin side up, on top. Cover with the remaining salt mixture and dill.

Cover with foil. Place a plate or oblong baking sheet or tin on top of the fish and weight it down, see Mrs Beeton's Tip, page 68. Leave in the refrigerator for 36 hours, during which time the salt mixture will become a brine solution. Turn the whole fillet 'sandwich' every day and baste with the liquor.

For the sauce, mix the mustard, sugar and dill. Add the oil very slowly, beating all the time to make a thick sauce. Stir in a little lemon juice with salt and pepper to taste.

Drain off the brine from the salmon and scrape away the dill and peppercorns before serving. Serve thinly sliced, garnished with fresh dill. Offer the mustard sauce separately.

SERVES 4 TO 6

Chicken or Turkey Mousse

Delicate Melba toast goes well with this mousse if it is served
for a light first course; for a more substantial luncheon dish, make
wholemeal toast and serve it hot with the mousse.

FOOD VALUES	TOTAL	PER PORTION
Protein	97g	24g
Carbohydrate	20g	5g
Fat	20g	5g
Fibre	—	—
kcals	649	262

225 g / 8 oz skinned cooked
  chicken or turkey breast
  meat
275 ml / 9 fl oz Chicken
  Stock (page 20), with fat
  removed
15 ml / 1 tbsp gelatine
2 egg yolks, beaten
salt and pepper
300 ml / ½ pint fromage
  frais, chilled

GARNISH
watercress sprigs
small lettuce leaves

Mince the poultry finely and put it in a bowl. Chill a second bowl. Put 100 ml / 3½ fl oz of the stock in a heatproof bowl, sprinkle on the gelatine and set aside for 15 minutes until spongy. Put the rest of the stock in the top of a double saucepan and stir in the beaten egg yolks, with salt and pepper to taste.

Place the pan over simmering water and cook gently, stirring frequently, until the mixture thickens slightly. Remove from the heat and pour into the chilled bowl. Stand the bowl containing the gelatine over a saucepan of hot water and stir the gelatine until it has dissolved completely. Stir into the egg mixture, mixing well. Add the minced chicken or turkey and stir until thoroughly mixed.

Stand the bowl in a basin of cold water or crushed ice, or place in the refrigerator until the mousse mixture begins to thicken at the edges. Fold in the chilled fromage frais. Turn into a wetted 1 litre / 1¾ pint mould and chill until set. To serve, turn out on to a platter and garnish with watercress and lettuce.

SERVES 4

Chaudfroid of Chicken

Chaudfroid of chicken may be made with portions (boneless breast portions, neat thigh joints or meaty quarters) or with a whole bird. For an elegant starter, use half a boneless chicken breast per person. This recipe illustrates the method of preparing a chaudfroid coating based on fromage frais instead of the traditional mayonnaise. Alternatively, the coating may be made using a Béchamel Sauce. Whichever coating is used, it is important to ensure that it is evenly applied and attractively garnished before serving.

FOOD VALUES	TOTAL	PER PORTION
Protein	148g	25g
Carbohydrate	17g	3g
Fat	42g	7g
Fibre	3g	1g
kcals	1034	172

6 *cooked chicken joints*
125 *ml / 4 fl oz aspic jelly*
  (*see below*)
200 *ml / 7 fl oz fromage frais*
lettuce leaves
3 *celery sticks, sliced*
2 *hard-boiled eggs, sliced*

GARNISH
stoned olives
tomato slices

Remove the skin, excess fat and any bones from the chicken joints, keeping the pieces in neat shapes. Chill the chicken joints until required. Melt the aspic jelly and leave to cool. When it is on the point of setting but still tepid, whisk in the fromage frais until smooth.

Place the chicken portions on a wire rack. As soon as the fromage frais mixture reaches a good coating consistency, pour it over the chicken portions to coat thoroughly.

Arrange the lettuce leaves on a serving dish and place the chicken portions on top. Surround with celery and hard-boiled egg slices and garnish with the olives and tomatoes.

MAKING ASPIC

To make 500 ml / 17 fl oz aspic jelly you require 500 ml / 17 fl oz chicken stock from which all fat has been removed. Remove all traces of grease from a large enamel or stainless steel saucepan by scalding it in boiling water. Also scald a piece of clean muslin, a metal sieve and a whisk. Put the stock into the pan with 60 ml / 4 tbsp white wine, 15 ml / 1 tbsp white wine vinegar, 20-25 g / ¾-1 oz gelatine, 1 bouquet garni and the white and crushed shell of 1 egg. Heat gently, whisking, until the gelatine dissolves, then bring the liquid to just below boiling point, whisking constantly. A thick white foam crust will form on top of the liquid. When this happens, remove the pan from the heat so that the foam falls back into the pan. Heat the stock in the same way one or twice more, until the liquid is crystal clear. Line the sieve with muslin and place it over a perfectly clean bowl. Strain the crust and liquid through the muslin into the bowl, trying not to break the crust. The aspic should be sparkling clear. If necessary, repeat the process, scalding the equipment again. Use aspic as directed in recipes or freeze in clean containers.

SERVES 6

Turkey Loaf

Neatly sliced and arranged on a platter, this loaf can be presented with a selection of other cold dishes as part of a mixed hors d'oeuvre. It is also perfect for family suppers, when it goes well with baked potatoes and a salad or baked beans.

FOOD VALUES	TOTAL	PER PORTION (6)
Protein	90g	15g
Carbohydrate	73g	12g
Fat	51g	9g
Fibre	5g	1g
kcals	1088	181

fat for greasing
50 g / 2 oz long-grain rice
225 g / 8 oz cooked turkey meat
4 rindless bacon rashers
salt and pepper
1 onion, finely chopped
about 50 ml / 2 fl oz turkey stock or Chicken Stock (page 20)
grated rind and juice of ½ lemon
50 g / 2 oz fresh wholemeal breadcrumbs
2.5 ml / ½ tsp chopped fresh thyme
5 ml / 1 tsp chopped parsley
15 ml / 1 tbsp milk

Grease a 450 g / 1 lb loaf tin. Set the oven at 190°C / 375°F / gas 5. Cook the rice in a saucepan of boiling salted water for 20 minutes, then drain and set aside.

Mince the turkey meat with the bacon. Put the mixture in a bowl and add plenty of salt and pepper. Stir in the onion, stock, lemon rind and rice.

In a separate bowl, mix the breadcrumbs, thyme, parsley and lemon juice. Add a little salt and pepper and mix in the milk to bind this stuffing.

Put half the turkey mixture in the prepared tin, spread with the stuffing, then cover with the remaining turkey mixture. Bake for about 35 minutes, until firm and browned on top. Turn out and serve hot or cold.

SERVES 6 TO 8

PATES,
TERRINES
AND POTTED
DISHES

MAKING PATES AND TERRINES AND POTTED DISHES

Home-made pâtés and potted foods have a character of their own, quite different from bought types and definitely superior to the majority of commercial varieties. With careful preparation, prompt cooling and chilling, they keep well in the refrigerator – ideal for serving as starters or savouries.

A pâté is a coarse or fine mixture, seasoned and flavoured for serving cold. Fish, meat, offal, poultry, game, cheese, vegetables or pulses may be potted or used to make pâtés. The term 'terrine' may be used to describe a lidded baking dish and, traditionally, a coarse pâté which is cooked in such a dish. Terrine is also now more broadly used for vegetable, fish or fruit recipes which are baked or set in a loaf-shaped container. Potted foods may be finely minced, cut up or whole, as in the case of shrimps, and served as for pâtés.

Preparation Techniques

Mincing or Puréeing When this is carried out depends on the recipe. Some pâtés require the raw meat, offal, onions and bread to be processed until smooth, then combined and cooked. Other recipes parcook the meat or offal before processing. Potted foods are usually cooked, if necessary, before being puréed. A mincer is the best appliance for puréeing raw meat, whereas a food processor or blender may be used for parcooked or cooked meat. Use a coarse blade first, followed by a fine one. For a very smooth result, sieve the purée.

Stretching Bacon for Lining Some pâtés are cooked in a tin, terrine or dish which is first lined with bacon rashers. Streaky bacon should be used and the rashers should be stretched with the back of a knife. When they are thin and long, lay them in the dish, overlapping each rasher and leaving extra length overhanging the edge. When the dish is filled with pâté, the ends of the bacon should be folded over the top of the mixture.

Baking in a Bain Marie To prevent the outside of the pâté from overcooking before the centre has cooked, the dish or container is placed in a roasting tin. Hot water is poured into the roasting tin to just below its rim, and the pâté is then baked. The water should be topped up during cooking.

Weighting To give the pâté its characteristic dense texture it should be weighted after cooking. Cover the top of the pâté with greaseproof paper and foil, then place a heavy weight on top. If the pâté has been cooked in a round dish, place a plate on top before adding the weight; the plate should be slightly smaller in diameter than the dish. Leave until cold, then chill overnight. Cans of food, scale weights or other suitably heavy items may be used to weight the pâté. A house brick wrapped in paper and a polythene bag also works well. Stand the dish in an outer container to catch any juices.

Storage and Usage Always keep pâtés and potted foods covered on a low shelf in the refrigerator. Remove slices or portions as required and return the rest to the refrigerator promptly. Most pâtés improve if they are allowed to mature for 1-2 days, but they should be eaten within a week. Pâtés made from poultry livers are the exception; they should be made and eaten within 2 days.

Liver Pâté

Serve this flavoursome pâté in the dish in which it was cooked, with hot dry toast, or cut into slices and serve with salad.

FOOD VALUES	TOTAL
Protein	120g
Carbohydrate	6g
Fat	145g
Fibre	—
kcals	1807

fat for greasing
75 g / 3 oz butter
100 g / 4 oz lean rindless
  bacon rashers, chopped
225 g / 8 oz calf's or pig's
  liver, trimmed and
  chopped
225 g / 8 oz chicken livers,
  trimmed and chopped
1 small onion, finely
  chopped
a few gherkins, chopped
  (optional)
1-2 hard-boiled eggs,
  chopped
salt and pepper
5-10 ml / 1-2 tsp dried
  mixed herbs

Grease an ovenproof terrine or similar dish. Set the oven at 180°C / 350°F / gas 4. Melt the butter in a frying pan, add the bacon, livers and onion and fry gently for 5-6 minutes. Mince finely twice or process in a blender or food processor to a smooth paste. Add the chopped gherkins and hard-boiled eggs, with salt, pepper and herbs to taste. Stir well. Spoon into the prepared dish; cover with buttered greaseproof paper.

Stand the dish in a roasting tin and add enough hot water to come to within 2.5 cm / 1 inch of the rim of the dish. Bake for 30 minutes.

When cooked, cover immediately and leave to cool, then chill before serving. Alternatively, the pâté may be pressed under a light weight for a closer texture when cooled and chilled.

MAKES ABOUT 675 G / 1½ LB

69

Herring Roe Pâté

FOOD VALUES	TOTAL
Protein	28g
Carbohydrate	7g
Fat	17g
Fibre	—
kcals	287

100 g / 4 oz soft herring roes
salt and pepper
25 g / 1 oz butter
50 g / 2 oz low-fat soft cheese
30 ml / 2 tbsp lemon juice
15 ml / 1 tbsp chopped
  parsley
chopped lettuce to garnish

Sprinkle the herring roes with salt and pepper. Melt the butter in a small frying pan, add the roes and fry gently for 10 minutes. Process the roes to a smooth paste in a blender or food processor, or pound them with a pestle in a mortar.

Add the soft cheese to the roe mixture, with the lemon juice and parsley. Turn into a small dish or mould and chill for 2 hours or until firm.

Turn out of the mould or serve from the dish. Garnish with the chopped lettuce and serve with fingers of hot dry toast or fresh brown bread.

MAKES ABOUT 175 G / 6 OZ

VARIATIONS

Herbed Herring Roe Pâté Use 30 ml / 2 tbsp chopped fresh dill instead of the parsley and add 15 ml / 1 tbsp snipped chives.
Herring Roe and Prawn Pâté Prepare the pâté as above. Roughly chop 100 g / 4 oz peeled cooked prawns and add them to the pâté before putting in the mould. Garnish with whole cooked prawns, if liked.

Baked Hare Pâté

FOOD VALUES	TOTAL
Protein	146g
Carbohydrate	21g
Fat	103g
Fibre	1g
kcals	1791

fat for greasing
1 thick slice of white bread,
    crust removed
15 ml / 1 tbsp milk
65 g / 2½ oz butter
50 g / 2 oz flat mushrooms,
    sliced
450 g / 1 lb cooked boneless
    hare meat, chopped
2 egg yolks
60-90 ml / 4-6 tbsp cooking
    brandy, Marsala or
    Madeira
gravy to moisten (optional)
salt and pepper
1 bay leaf to garnish

Soak the bread in the milk in a shallow bowl for 10 minutes. Meanwhile melt 15 g / ½ oz of the butter in a small frying pan, add the mushrooms and fry gently until soft.

Mash the bread lightly and put it in the bowl of a blender or food processor with the mushrooms and hare meat. Process finely. Scrape the mixture into a bowl, using a rubber spatula.

Melt the remaining butter and stir it into the bowl with the egg yolks and liquor. Moisten with a little gravy if necessary and add salt and pepper to taste.

Set the oven 160°C / 325°F / gas 3. Grease a terrine or pie dish. Centre the bay leaf on the base of the dish, scrape in the hare mixture and cover the dish tightly with foil.

Stand the terrine or dish in a roasting tin. Pour boiling water into the outer tin to come almost up to the rim of the dish. Bake the pâté for 2 hours, then weight and cool it. Chill for 12 hours. To serve, turn out on to a platter so that the bay leaf is on top. Serve in thin slices.

MAKES ABOUT 300 G / 11 OZ

Pork Brawn

Although the idea of cooking a pig's head may be anathema to modern cooks, the butcher prepares the 'joint' beyond immediate recognition and it is worth the effort of cooking brawn to experience the full flavour of meat jellied in an aromatic stock.

FOOD VALUES	TOTAL	PER PORTION (4)
Protein	147g	37g
Carbohydrate	–	–
Fat	215g	54g
Fibre	–	–
kcals	2521	655

½ *pig's head, ears, brain*
  and snout removed
1 *pig's trotter, split*
350 *g / 12 oz shin of beef*
  (optional)
15 *ml / 1 tbsp salt*
6 *black peppercorns*
6 *cloves*
5 *ml / 1 tsp dried marjoram*
  or oregano
5 *ml / 1 tsp ground mace or*
  2 blades of mace
2 *bay leaves*
1 *large fresh sage sprig*
2 *fresh thyme sprigs*
1 *fresh rosemary sprig*
1 *fresh savory sprig*
  (optional)
4 *parsley sprigs, with long*
  stalks
2 *onions, cut into chunks*
2 *large carrots, sliced*
1 *small turnip, cubed*

Pig's heads are sold as part of the carcass, so any good butcher or supermarket which butchers its own meat (rather than taking prepacked deliveries) will be able to supply a head within a few days of ordering. Ask for the ears, snout and brain to be removed, and for the half head to be chopped into two pieces Have the trotter split in half.

Wash the head well in salted cold water, then rinse it under clear water and place the pieces in a large pan. Add the shin of beef, if used, the trotter, salt, peppercorns, cloves, marjoram and mace. Tie the bay leaves and herb sprigs into a neat bouquet garni and add them to the pan. A dried bouquet garni is no replacement for fresh herbs as their flavour is important. Add the onions, carrots and turnip to the pan, then pour in cold water to cover the meat amply. Bring to the boil, then use a slotted spoon to skim the surface of the liquid for the first 5-10 minutes' cooking, or until the scum has stopped forming. Take care to avoid removing any onion or too much of the dried herb and mace. Reduce the heat so that the liquid is just boiling and cover the pan. Cook for 3 hours.

Have a very large bowl or saucepan, metal colander and two large meat plates ready, then lift the head and shin, if used, from the pan on to one plate. A large fish slice and barbecue fork are ideal for this. Strain the cooking liquid through a colander into the bowl or pan. Replace the trotters in the bowl or pan but discard the vegetables and herbs. If the stock has been strained into a bowl, pour it back into the clean pan. Bring it just to the boil.

Transfer a piece of meat to the clean plate for preparation. Use a sharp pointed knife to cut off the rind, leaving a thin layer of fat over the meat. Cut all the meat off the bones, using the point of the knife to scrape the crevices – this is an easy task as the meat literally falls away from the carcass.

Do not discard all the fat as it contributes flavour and moistens the finished brawn; however, remove all blood vessels and any small, dark and hard portions that are offal-like in appearance and texture. The meat is easy to distinguish as it is quite stringy and plentiful. Cut the meat into small pieces, across the grain, and chop the fat. Return any bones to the pan of stock for further boiling. Trim any fat and gristle from the beef, if used, and chop the meat. Mix it with the pork.

Cook the stock with the bones in the open pan until well reduced to less than half its original volume, then strain it again. You should aim to reduce the stock to 1.1-1.25 litres / 2-2¼ pints as this concentrates the flavour and gives a firm brawn. Although further reduction will intensify the flavour, the resultant brawn would set more firmly than is desirable. Lastly, strain the stock through a sieve lined with scalded muslin.

Mix the pork and fat well with the beef, if used, and place it in a 1.1 litre / 2 pint basin. Stir in about 450 ml / ¾ pint of the strained stock, mixing well at first, until all the meat is evenly distributed and the top just covered with stock. Cover and cool, then chill for at least 3 hours, or until set.

SERVES 4 TO 6

MRS BEETON'S TIP

The leftover stock makes delicious soup or it may be used in casseroles: cool, then freeze it in usable quantities.

To serve, slide the point of a knife around the rim of the brawn, between it and the basin. Cover with a plate and invert both the basin and the plate, giving them a firm jerk to release the jellied meat. Cut into slices and serve the brawn with ripe tomatoes or salad and baked or fried potatoes. Alternatively, offer it with plain chunks of bread. Any leftover brawn makes a delicious sandwich filling.

Pork Cheese

This pâté-style recipe for cooked pork may be served with bread or toast and a salad as a lunchtime snack or supper dish. Scoop it out of the baking dish rather than attempt to unmould the mixture.

FOOD VALUES	TOTAL	PER PORTION (10)
Protein	219g	22g
Carbohydrate	16g	2g
Fat	498g	50g
Fibre	1g	–
kcals	5418	542

1.4 kg / 3 lb belly of pork, boned
salt and pepper
30 ml / 2 tbsp chopped parsley
5 ml / 1 tsp chopped fresh thyme or 2.5 ml / ½ tsp dried thyme
2.5 ml / ½ tsp chopped rosemary
15 ml / 1 tbsp chopped fresh sage or 5 ml / 1 tsp dried sage
2.5 ml / ½ tsp ground mace
a little grated nutmeg
grated rind of ½ lemon
300 ml / ½ pint pork gravy
butter for greasing

Set the oven at 180°C / 350°F / gas 4. Place the pork in a roasting tin and cook for 1½ hours, until cooked through. Leave to cool for about 30 minutes, or until just cool enough to handle.

Set the oven at 180°C / 350°F / gas 4 again. Cut all the rind off the pork. Chop the meat and fat, either by hand or in a food processor. Do not overprocess the mixture. Place the pork in a large bowl. Add plenty of salt and pepper, all the herbs, the mace, nutmeg and lemon rind. If you have a large pestle, use it to pound the meat with the flavouring ingredients; if not, use the back of a sturdy mixing spoon. The more you pound the mixture, the better the texture.

When all the ingredients are thoroughly mixed, work in the gravy to bind them together loosely. Good thick gravy is best as it will not make the mixture too runny, more can be incorporated and the cheese will have a good flavour.

Grease a 1.1 litre / 2 pint ovenproof dish, for example a soufflé dish or terrine. Turn the mixture into the dish, smooth it down and cover with foil. Bake for 1¼ hours, then leave to cool completely. Chill overnight before serving.

SERVES 10 TO 12

Terrine of Duck

A slice of duck terrine, served with a twist of orange and a simple salad garnish, makes an ideal starter.

FOOD VALUES	TOTAL
Protein	234g
Carbohydrate	4g
Fat	231g
Fibre	1g
kcals	3305

450 g / 1 lb boneless duck meat, minced

125 ml / 4 fl oz brandy

450 g / 1 lb thinly sliced pork back fat or rindless streaky bacon rashers

225 g / 8 oz rindless boned belly of pork

275 g / 10 oz boneless chicken breast

2 shallots, chopped

rind of 1 orange, cut into fine shreds

2.5 ml / ½ tsp dried thyme

salt and pepper

3 eggs, beaten

Put the duck meat into a large bowl with the brandy, cover and marinate for 4-6 hours.

Set the oven at 180°C / 350°F / gas 4. Line a 1.4 litre / 2½ pint ovenproof serving dish with slices of pork fat or bacon, reserving enough to cover the top of the dish.

Mince the belly of pork and chicken together, then add to the duck meat in the bowl. Stir in the shallots, orange rind and thyme, with salt and pepper to taste. Stir in the eggs and mix well. Spoon into the lined dish, smooth and level the surface and cover with the reserved fat or bacon.

Cover the dish with foil and stand the terrine in a roasting tin. Pour boiling water into the outer tin to come almost up to the rim of the dish. Bake for 1¼ hours, or until the terrine shrinks slightly from the sides of the dish and any melted fat on the top is clear. Remove the foil and top layer of fat 15 minutes before the end of cooking time to let the pâté brown slightly.

When cooked, weight the terrine. Cool, then chill for 12 hours. Serve in slices.

MAKES ABOUT 1.4 KG / 3 LB

Fish Terrine

This terrine may be served as a first course or as a light lunch or supper dish. Melba toast, crisp wholemeal toast or French bread are suitable accompaniments.

FOOD VALUES	TOTAL	PER PORTION
Protein	232g	29g
Carbohydrate	91g	11g
Fat	127g	16g
Fibre	2g	–
kcals	2410	302

450 g / 1 lb plaice fillets, skinned
225 g / 8 oz smoked salmon offcuts
50 g / 2 oz butter
50 g / 2 oz plain flour
600 ml / 1 pint milk
6 eggs
30 ml / 2 tbsp chopped parsley
30 ml / 2 tbsp snipped chives
salt and pepper

FROMAGE FRAIS AND CHIVE SAUCE
300 ml / ½ pint fromage frais
60 ml / 4 tbsp snipped chives

Set the oven at 160°C / 325°F / gas 3. Prepare a bain marie: have ready a large roasting tin or dish and a kettle of boiling water. Base line and grease a 900 g / 2 lb loaf tin.

Pick any tiny bones from the plaice and purée it in a food processor or blender. Transfer to a large bowl. Check that the smoked salmon offcuts are free of all bones and skin, then purée them and place in a separate, large bowl.

Melt the butter in a saucepan and stir in the flour. Cook over low heat for 2-3 minutes, without browning. With the heat on the lowest setting, gradually add the milk, stirring all the time. If lumps begin to form, stop pouring in liquid and stir vigorously until the sauce is smooth, then continue pouring in the milk. Bring the sauce to the boil, stirring, until thickened. Cover and allow to cool for 10 minutes.

Add half the sauce to the plaice purée, the remainder to the smoked salmon. Beat 3 eggs and stir them into the plaice mixture; beat the remaining eggs and add to the smoked salmon mixture. Stir the parsley into the plaice, the chives into the smoked salmon. Add salt and pepper to taste to the plaice mixture; pepper only to the smoked salmon mixture.

Spoon half the plaice mixture into the prepared tin. Top with the salmon mixture then the remaining plaice mixture. Cover with foil and stand the terrine in the roasting tin. Pour boiling water into the outer tin to come almost up to the rim. Bake the fish terrine in the bain marie for 1¼ hours, or until it feels firm to the touch. If the middle feels soft, continue cooking for 10-15 minutes more.

Meanwhile, mix the fromage frais with the chives. Add salt and pepper to taste, then cover and chill for at least an hour, so that the chives flavour the fromage frais.

Leave the cooked terrine to stand for 5 minutes before turning it out. Invert the tin on to a warmed platter. Serve in slices with the fromage frais and chive sauce. Alternatively, the terrine may be served cold, with Melba toast, if liked.

SERVES 8

Potted Herring Fillets

This makes an excellent starter with Melba toast, a flavoursome sandwich filling or a useful spread for serving with crusty bread as a light snack.

FOOD VALUES	TOTAL
Protein	33g
Carbohydrate	1g
Fat	30g
Fibre	—
kcals	405

1 (198 g / 7 oz) can herring
   fillets in tomato sauce
25 g / 1 oz butter
pinch of ground mace
salt and pepper

Mash the herring fillets with any sauce from the can. Melt the butter in a small saucepan. Add the mashed herrings, the mace and salt and pepper to taste. Stir until the mixture is just heated. Cool slightly, then turn into small pots. Cover and refrigerate until firm.

MAKES ABOUT 200 G / 7 OZ

Marbled Rabbit

FOOD VALUES	TOTAL	PER PORTION
Protein	389g	49g
Carbohydrate	111g	14g
Fat	108g	14g
Fibre	3g	–
kcals	2950	369

2 rabbits, jointed, liver and
   kidneys reserved
salt and pepper
450 g / 1 lb gammon or
   boiling bacon, sliced
1.1 litres / 2 pints Chicken
   Stock (page 20)
2.5 ml / ½ tsp dried mixed
   herbs
5 ml / 1 tsp chopped parsley
fresh white breadcrumbs (see
   method)
beaten egg to bind
fat for shallow frying
10 ml / 2 tsp gelatine
2 hard-boiled eggs, sliced

Put the rabbit joints into a shallow dish with strongly salted water to cover. Set aside for at least 1 hour. Rinse and drain thoroughly.

Chop half the gammon or bacon and set it aside. Pack the rabbit joints into a saucepan with the remaining gammon or bacon on top. Barely cover with stock. Cover the pan tightly. Simmer gently for 1¼-1½ hours, until the rabbit is tender. Check the level of the stock from time to time and top up as necessary.

Remove the rabbit joints with a slotted spoon. Cut the meat off the bones and chop it into large pieces. Trim into neat shapes and set aside. Reserve the trimmings. Strain the stock into a clean saucepan. Finely chop any gammon or bacon pieces remaining in the strainer; put them in a bowl. Finely chop the reserved trimmings and add them to the bowl with the herbs. Add salt and pepper to taste. Weigh the mixture and add half its weight in breadcrumbs. Mix well. Bind the mixture with beaten egg and form into small forcemeat balls.

Add the remaining stock to the saucepan, bring to simmering point and poach the forcemeat balls for 10 minutes. Remove with a slotted spoon, drain and set aside.

Trim the rabbit liver and kidneys. Heat the fat for shallow frying in a small frying pan, add the liver and kidneys and fry until just tender. Remove with a

78

slotted spoon and slice. Add the reserved chopped gammon or bacon to the fat remaining in the pan; fry until cooked.

Strain 300 ml / ½ pint of the stock into a small bowl. Sprinkle the gelatine on to the liquid. Set aside until spongy, then stand the bowl over a saucepan of hot water; stir until the gelatine has dissolved completely. Allow to cool but not set.

Pour a little of the gelatine mixture into a wetted mould. Chill until set. Cover with pieces of rabbit, layered with the fried gammon or bacon, the forcemeat balls, slices of liver and kidney and slices of hard-boiled egg. Do not pack down tightly; fill up the mould with the remaining gelatine mixture, covering the ingredients completely. Chill for 3-4 hours until set, then turn out on to a serving dish.

SERVES 8

NUTRITION NOTE

Both wild and farmed rabbits yield lean meat which is well suited to healthy eating. Available as neat portions on the bone, or boned and diced, rabbit meat may be used in a variety of dishes, such as stir fries, casseroles, pies and braised dishes. Small portions are also suitable for grilling or barbecuing.

Rabbit Terrine

FOOD VALUES	TOTAL
Protein	340g
Carbohydrate	3g
Fat	346g
Fibre	–
kcals	4654

2 oven-ready pigeons
1 (1 kg / 2¼ lb) rabbit, skinned and boned or 450 g / 1 lb boneless rabbit meat
100 g / 4 oz pig's liver, trimmed and sliced
150 ml / ¼ pint red wine
1 bay leaf
275 g / 10 oz unsmoked rindless streaky bacon rashers
450 g / 1 lb rindless boned belly of pork, coarsely chopped
1 garlic clove, crushed
30 ml / 2 tbsp brandy
freshly ground black pepper

Remove the pigeon meat from the bones and place in a mixing bowl with the rabbit meat. Add the liver, wine and bay leaf. Cover tightly and marinate overnight in the refrigerator.

Stretch the bacon rashers lightly with the back of a knife and line a 2 litre / 3½ pint terrine or pie dish. Set the oven at 160°C / 325°F / gas 3.

Drain the meat, reserving the marinade. Mince the pork and marinated meats or process roughly in a food processor. Stir in the garlic, reserved marinade and brandy. Season with plenty of black pepper.

Spoon the mixture into the prepared terrine and cover with foil or a lid. Stand the dish in a roasting tin and add enough hot water to come to within 2.5 cm / 1 inch of the rim of the tin. Bake for about 2 hours.

When cooked, pour off any excess liquid and weight the pâté. Cool, then chill before serving.

MAKES ABOUT 1.6 KG / 3½ LB

Chicken Jelly

Set the jelly in six ramekins for serving as a starter.

FOOD VALUES	TOTAL	PER PORTION (6)
Protein	147g	25g
Carbohydrate	—	—
Fat	31g	5g
Fibre	—	—
kcals	872	145

1.5 litres / 2¾ pints
   Vegetable Stock (*page*
   20)
1 (1.1 kg / 2½ lb) chicken,
   skinned and jointed
2 celery sticks, sliced
1 onion, thickly sliced
1 carrot, thickly sliced
salt
15 ml / 1 tbsp white wine
   vinegar
2 bay leaves
5 peppercorns
white and crushed shell of
   1 egg
30 ml / 2 tbsp gelatine

Bring the stock to the boil in a large saucepan. Put in the chicken pieces, vegetables, salt, vinegar, bay leaves and peppercorns. Bring back to the boil and skim well. Lower the heat, cover the pan and simmer the chicken for 45 minutes until tender. Using a slotted spoon, remove the chicken pieces. Cut the meat off the bones in small pieces, cool and chill. Return the bones to the stock in the pan and boil until reduced by half. Strain, cool and chill the stock. Skim off the fat.

Scald a large enamel or stainless steel (not aluminium) saucepan, a piece of clean muslin or thin white cotton, a metal sieve and a whisk in boiling water. Pour the stock into the pan with the egg white, crushed shell and gelatine. Bring to the boil over moderate heat, whisking constantly with the whisk until a thick white crust of foam develops on the top of the liquid. Remove the whisk. As soon as the liquid rises to the top of the pan, remove it from the heat. Leave to stand briefly until the foam falls back into the pan, then heat the stock in the same way once or twice more, until the stock is crystal clear. Strain the stock through the muslin-lined sieve into a perfectly clean bowl.

Arrange the reserved chicken meat in a wetted 1 litre / 1¾ pint mould. Pour the stock over gently. Cool, then chill. Turn out to serve.

SERVES 6 TO 8

Potted Mushrooms

Serve full-flavoured potted mushrooms with crackers as a
starter, or with thick slices of Granary bread and a crisp green salad
for a light lunch or supper.

FOOD VALUES	TOTAL	PER PORTION
Protein	11g	3g
Carbohydrate	2g	1g
Fat	45g	11g
Fibre	5g	1g
kcals	455	116

*450 g / 1 lb mushrooms,
  finely chopped
50 g / 2 oz butter
salt and pepper
pinch of ground allspice
2 anchovy fillets, finely
  mashed*

Place the mushrooms in a heavy-bottomed
saucepan over gentle heat until the juice runs
freely. Raise the heat and cook, uncovered, stirring
often until all the juice evaporates and the
mushrooms are dry.

Add the butter with salt and pepper to taste.
Sprinkle with the allspice and continue cooking for
about 5 minutes, or until all the butter is absorbed.

Stir in the anchovies and cook for 2 minutes more.
Remove from the heat, turn into small pots and
leave to cool. Cover and chill for at least an hour
before serving.

MAKES ABOUT 300 G / 11 OZ OR SERVES 4

Potted Game

A small amount of game, potted with cooked ham or bacon,
makes a satisfying starter. Alternatively, try it with salad as the
basis of a light lunch or picnic.

FOOD VALUES	TOTAL
Protein	131g
Carbohydrate	–
Fat	99g
Fibre	–
kcals	1418

350 g / 12 oz cooked
  boneless game meat,
  trimmed
100 g / 4 oz cooked ham or
  boiled bacon, trimmed
75 g / 3 oz butter, softened
pinch of cayenne pepper
salt
1.25 ml / ¼ tsp ground
  black pepper

GARNISH
bay leaves
juniper berries

Mince the game and ham or bacon very finely.
Pound it to a smooth paste, gradually working in
the butter. Alternatively, grind the meats in a food
processor; add the butter and process briefly to
combine. Mix in the cayenne, with salt and pepper.

Turn the mixture into small pots. Garnish with bay
leaves and juniper berries. Cover. Refrigerate the
pots until the mixture is firm.

MAKES ABOUT 450 G / 1 LB

LIGHT DIPS AND CRUNCHY CRUDITES

Serving one or two dips is a good alternative to providing a formal first course for a meal, especially when the main course is a substantial roast or if you plan a spectacularly luscious dessert. Dips and nibbles are also firm favourites for parties and they can also make a delicious informal lunch or supper.

Thick and Creamy Vegetable Dips

Smooth low-fat soft cheese – such as light Philadelphia cheese or any of the similar products – is a good base for making a thick, creamy dip. Peeled, seeded and diced tomatoes will soften the consistency of the cheese for dipping, or a little fromage frais or yogurt may be stirred in.

Celery, spring onions, carrots and red or green pepper are tasty flavouring ingredients. Make sure they are very finely and evenly diced (not quite chopped) so that they impart all their flavour to the dip and give it just the right texture. Season vegetable dips with a dash of anchovy paste, a little mushroom ketchup, tomato purée (and a pinch of sugar), a little grated nutmeg, a sprinkling of paprika or a little cayenne pepper.

Serve firm dippers with creamy mixtures. For example, carrot, pepper and celery sticks, radishes, button mushrooms, large croûtons, breadsticks and small crackers.

Light Herb Dips

Curd cheese, medium-fat soft cheese and sieved cottage cheese all make softer bases than the firmer-textured low-fat soft cheeses. Fold in fromage frais to give a light, delicate yet creamy dip.

Chopped parsley, tarragon, mint and chervil provide a delicate flavour. Snipped chives make a delicious dip without any additional flavouring ingredients. Basil and watercress are also delicious in light dips. It is best to avoid the slightly tough or extremely pungent herbs, such as rosemary, savory and thyme, which can be a little overpowering.

Seasoning is important as without any salt and pepper herb dips can be rather bland. Paprika and nutmeg are also useful.

Soft, light cheese dips are also perfect for serving with the more fragile accompaniments which snap easily – small squares of Melba toast, light crisps and pieces of poppadom.

Substantial Dips

Beans and pulses make terrific dips which can be served hot as well as cold. A base of finely chopped onion, sautéed with some garlic in a little oil, can be mixed with mashed cooked or canned red kidney beans, chick peas, borlotti beans or butter beans.

Spicy seasonings are excellent with these ingredients – ground coriander, cumin, turmeric, curry powder or garam masala should be lightly cooked with the onion. Tomato purée, Worcestershire sauce, mushroom ketchup and mustard are also suitable seasonings.

For lighter flavours, grated lemon rind, sesame seeds or tahini (sesame paste) are the perfect choice. Cooked and mashed red lentils and chick peas are particularly good pulses to use with these ingredients.

Fromage frais and yogurt can be added to soften the mixture to a dipping consistency.

These dips may be turned into quite satisfying snacks by serving warm pitta bread, Bath Oliver biscuits or water biscuits as dippers.

Taramasalata

A food processor may be used to make taramasalata.

FOOD VALUES	TOTAL	PER PORTION
Protein	6g	2g
Carbohydrate	8g	2g
Fat	88g	22g
Fibre	–	–
kcals	847	212

100 g / 4 oz smoked cod's roe, skinned
1 garlic clove, halved
30 ml / 2 tbsp lemon juice
60 ml / 4 tbsp olive oil
black pepper
pitta bread, lemon wedges and black olives, to serve

Using a mortar and pestle, pound the cod's roe and garlic with the lemon juice until smooth. Add the olive oil and 30 ml / 2 tbsp water alternately in small amounts, beating well after each addition, until the paste is smooth and completely blended. Grind in black pepper to taste and serve with warm pitta bread, lemon wedges and olives.

SERVES 4

NUTRITION NOTE

Olive oil is rich in monounsaturated fats which, it is recommended, may make up to a maximum of 17 per cent of the diet's energy supply. In total, fat should not exceed 35 per cent of the energy intake, of which saturated fats should not exceed 10 per cent and polyunsaturated fats 8 per cent.

Quick Tomato Dip

FOOD VALUES	TOTAL	PER PORTION
Protein	35g	9g
Carbohydrate	14g	4g
Fat	10g	3g
Fibre	2g	1g
kcals	285	71

225 g / 8 oz cottage cheese
30 ml / 2 tbsp tomato purée
45 ml / 3 tbsp snipped chives
30 ml / 2 tbsp chopped
  parsley
15 ml / 1 tbsp creamed
  horseradish
30 ml / 2 tbsp fromage frais
salt and pepper

Press the cottage cheese through a fine sieve or process it in a blender or food processor until smooth – take care not to overprocess the cheese so that it becomes runny. Mix in the tomato purée, chives, parsley and creamed horseradish, then fold in the fromage frais. Stir in salt and pepper to taste and place in a serving bowl. Cover and chill for at least an hour before serving.

SERVES 4

Celery and Ham Dip

FOOD VALUES	TOTAL	PER PORTION
Protein	42g	11g
Carbohydrate	12g	3g
Fat	40g	10g
Fibre	1g	—
kcals	572	143

2 celery sticks
225 g / 8 oz curd cheese
100 g / 4 oz cooked ham,
  finely chopped
2 spring onions, chopped
15-30 ml / 1-2 tbsp fromage
  frais
salt and pepper
grated nutmeg
paprika

Cut the celery sticks lengthways into fine strips, then across into small dice. Stir the celery into the curd cheese with the ham and spring onions, then fold in the fromage frais to soften the mixture. Add seasoning to taste, a little nutmeg and paprika, then turn the mixture into a serving dish. Cover and chill for at least an hour before serving.

SERVES 4

HOT STARTERS AND SAVOURIES

Hot Stuffed Avocados

A useful starter for a winter's dinner or for a special light lunch.

FOOD VALUES	TOTAL	PER PORTION
Protein	67g	17g
Carbohydrate	25g	6g
Fat	121g	30g
Fibre	21g	5g
kcals	1450	365

2 large avocados
100 g / 4 oz cooked smoked
* haddock or cod*
50 g / 2 oz ricotta cheese
lemon juice
salt and pepper
chopped parsley
about 25 g / 1 oz fresh white
* breadcrumbs*
grated lemon rind to garnish

Set the oven at 200°C / 400°F / gas 6. Cut the avocados in half lengthways and remove the stones.

Flake the fish and mix with the ricotta. Fill the hollows of the avocados with the fish mixture. Sprinkle the surface of the avocado and fish with lemon juice, and season the avocado only with a sprinkling of salt and pepper. Stir some parsley into the breadcrumbs, then spoon over the avocados.

Place the avocados in a baking dish. Bake for 15-20 minutes. Garnish with lemon. Serve at once.

SERVES 4

Avocado Ramekins

These individual savoury soufflés make a spectacular start to a special meal.

FOOD VALUES	TOTAL	PER PORTION
Protein	26g	7g
Carbohydrate	18g	5g
Fat	74g	19g
Fibre	5g	1g
kcals	841	210

oil for greasing
50 ml / 2 fl oz milk
about 25 g / 1 oz fresh white
  breadcrumbs
50 g / 2 oz Cheshire or
  Cheddar cheese, finely
  grated
25 g / 1 oz unsalted butter,
  melted
1 egg, separated
1 avocado, halved, stoned,
  peeled and finely diced
salt and pepper
pinch of ground mace

Grease four small ovenproof pots or ramekins. Set the oven at 200°C / 400°F / gas 6.

Heat the milk and pour it over the breadcrumbs to cover them. Leave to stand for 5-10 minutes. Stir in the cheese and butter. Beat the yolk into the cheese mixture. Add the avocado, with salt, pepper and mace to taste. Mix lightly.

In a clean, grease-free bowl, whisk the egg white until stiff. Using a metal spoon, stir one spoonful of the egg white into the cheese mixture to lighten it, then fold in the rest. Spoon into the prepared pots or ramekins.

Bake for 25-30 minutes until risen and lightly browned. Serve immediately.

SERVES 4

Peperonata

A delicious starter from Italy, peperonata is perfect for
serving with prosciutto or salami.

FOOD VALUES	TOTAL	PER PORTION
Protein	10g	3g
Carbohydrate	57g	14g
Fat	49g	12g
Fibre	16g	4g
kcals	695	174

45 ml / 3 tbsp olive oil
1 large onion, sliced
2 garlic cloves, crushed
350 g / 12 oz tomatoes,
  peeled, seeded and cut in
  quarters
2 large red peppers, seeded
  and cut in thin strips
1 large green pepper, seeded
  and cut in thin strips
1 large yellow pepper, seeded
  and cut in thin strips
2.5 ml / ½ tsp coriander
  seeds, lightly crushed
  (optional)
salt and pepper
15 ml / 1 tbsp red wine
  vinegar (optional)

Heat the oil in a large frying pan, add the onion and
garlic and fry over gentle heat for 10 minutes. Add
the tomatoes, peppers and coriander seeds, if used,
with salt and pepper to taste.

Cover and cook gently for 1 hour, stirring from time
to time. Add more salt and pepper before serving if
necessary. To sharpen the flavour, stir in the red
wine vinegar, if liked.

SERVES 4

NUTRITION NOTE

Fresh raw peppers are particularly rich in vitamin C. In general, to optimize the
vitamin contribution which fresh fruit and vegetables make to the diet, ensure
that they are as fresh as possible, use a stainless steel knife in preparation and
shred leafy vegetables which are to be cooked as little as possible. Lastly, cook
vegetables in the minimum amount of water and for the shortest possible
time. Never add bicarbonate of soda to cooking water. Use the cooking liquid
for gravy, sauce or soup.

Spanish Prawns

Supply paper napkins and finger bowls for this dish and don't
forget a plate for the prawn shells.

FOOD VALUES	TOTAL	PER PORTION
Protein	39g	10g
Carbohydrate	–	–
Fat	78g	20g
Fibre	–	–
kcals	894	224

75 ml / 5 tbsp olive oil
1 garlic clove, crushed
1 small bunch of chives,
   snipped
450 g / 1 lb whole cooked
   prawns
30 ml / 2 tbsp dry sherry
salt and pepper

Heat the oil in a large frying pan. Stir in the garlic
and chives. Add the prawns and sherry, with salt
and pepper to taste.

Cover the pan and cook over moderate heat for 3-5
minutes, turning the prawns over once. Serve in
small bowls, with crusty French bread, if liked.

SERVES 4

Scalloped Cod's Roe

FOOD VALUES	TOTAL	PER PORTION
Protein	97g	24g
Carbohydrate	48g	12g
Fat	85g	21g
Fibre	1g	–
kcals	1337	334

fat for greasing
400 g / 14 oz smoked cod's
  roe, skinned
salt
white wine vinegar
45 ml / 3 tbsp reduced-fat
  single cream
browned breadcrumbs, see
  Mrs Beeton's Tip

SAUCE
25 g / 1 oz butter
25 g / 1 oz plain flour
300 ml / ½ pint milk
salt and pepper
15 ml / 1 tbsp chopped
  parsley

Make the sauce. Melt the butter in a saucepan. Stir in the flour and cook over a low heat for 2-3 minutes, without allowing the mixture to colour. Gradually add the milk, stirring constantly until the sauce boils and thickens. Add salt and pepper to taste. Stir in the parsley. Cover the surface of the sauce with damp greaseproof paper and set aside.

Grease four scallop shells. Set the oven at 200°C / 400°F / gas 6. Put the cod's roe in a saucepan with water to cover. Flavour the water with a little salt and vinegar and bring to simmering point. Poach the cod's roe for 10 minutes, remove with a slotted spoon and set aside on a plate until tepid; the roe will firm up.

Chop the cod's roe and add it to the parsley sauce with the cream. Mix lightly. Divide the cod's roe mixture between the prepared scallop shells, top with the browned breadcrumbs and place on a baking sheet. Bake for 2-3 minutes or until the sauce bubbles and the browned breadcrumbs are crisp.

SERVES 4

MRS BEETON'S TIP

Browned breadcrumbs – or raspings as they were called in Mrs Beeton's day – are an ideal way of using up bread crusts or bread that has begun to stale. Spread them on a baking sheet and bake at 180°C / 350°F / gas 4 until golden brown and crisp. Crush with a rolling pin or in a blender or food processor. Use for coating croquettes, fish cakes or rissoles, or for topping gratins.

Devilled Herring Roes

FOOD VALUES	TOTAL	PER PORTION (4)
Protein	60g	15g
Carbohydrate	95g	24g
Fat	58g	15g
Fibre	3g	1g
kcals	1119	280

200 g / 7 oz soft herring roes
30 ml / 2 tbsp plain flour
salt and pepper
15 ml / 1 tbsp oil
50 g / 2 oz butter, softened
3 anchovy fillets, mashed
lemon juice
4 slices of bread
cayenne pepper
paprika

Rinse the herring roes. Spread the flour in a shallow bowl, add salt and pepper to taste and roll the herring roes lightly in the seasoned flour until coated.

Heat the oil and half the butter in a frying pan, add the floured roes and fry for about 10 minutes until golden brown all over. Remove the roes with a slotted spoon and drain on absorbent kitchen paper. Set the frying pan aside.

Mix the remaining butter with the anchovy fillets in a small bowl. Add a dash of lemon juice and a little black pepper to taste. Toast the bread and cut off the crusts. Cut each slice in half and spread with the anchovy butter. Arrange the roes on the buttered toast and place in a heated dish.

Add a good squeeze of lemon juice and a pinch of cayenne to the frying pan. Heat for a couple of seconds, then scrape the mixture over the roes, dust with paprika and serve very hot.

SERVES 8 AS A STARTER; 4 AS A SNACK OR LIGHT MEAL

Scallops on Skewers

FOOD VALUES	TOTAL	PER PORTION
Protein	160g	40g
Carbohydrate	33g	8g
Fat	207g	52g
Fibre	11g	3g
kcals	2627	657

12 *shallots or small onions,*
   peeled but left whole
2 *courgettes cut in 2 cm /*
   ¾ inch cubes
8 *rindless bacon rashers*
16 *scallops*
12 *button mushrooms*
15 *ml / 1 tbsp oil*
salt and pepper

Put the shallots or onions in a small saucepan with water to cover. Bring to the boil, lower the heat and simmer for 4 minutes. Add the courgettes and simmer for 2 minutes more. Drain thoroughly.

Stretch the bacon over the back of a knife and cut each rasher in half. Wrap half a rasher around each scallop. Thread the onions, courgettes, mushrooms and bacon-wrapped scallops alternately on four skewers.

Brush the oil over the kebabs. Sprinkle with salt and pepper to taste. Grill under moderate heat for 5-7 minutes, turning frequently. Serve at once.

SERVES 4

Monkfish and Bacon Kebabs

FOOD VALUES	TOTAL	PER PORTION
Protein	175g	29g
Carbohydrate	1g	–
Fat	224g	37g
Fibre	2g	–
kcals	2714	452

125 ml / 4 fl oz olive oil
1 garlic clove, crushed
5 ml / 1 tsp lemon juice
5 ml / 1 tsp dried oregano
800 g / 1¾ lb monkfish,
  cleaned, trimmed and cut
  into 2 cm / ¾ inch cubes
225 g / 8 oz rindless bacon
  rashers
200 g / 7 oz small
  mushrooms
salt and pepper

Combine the olive oil, garlic, lemon juice and oregano in a shallow bowl large enough to hold all the monkfish cubes in a single layer. Mix well, add the fish, and marinate for 15 minutes. Drain the monkfish, reserving the marinade.

Thread a piece of bacon on to a kebab skewer. Add a cube of fish, then a mushroom, weaving the bacon between them. Continue to add the fish and mushrooms, each time interweaving the bacon, until the skewer is full. Add a second rasher of bacon if necessary. Fill five more skewers in the same way. Sprinkle with salt and pepper.

Grill the monkfish kebabs under moderate heat for 10-15 minutes, basting frequently with the reserved marinade.

SERVES 6

NUTRITION NOTE

White fish is a low-fat source of high-quality protein; in addition it is also a useful source of iodine.

Coquilles St Jacques Mornay

Great care must be taken not to overcook the scallops. Their delectable flavour and texture is easily spoiled by high heat.

FOOD VALUES	TOTAL	PER PORTION
Protein	111g	28g
Carbohydrate	133g	33g
Fat	41g	10g
Fibre	9g	2g
kcals	1336	334

450 g / 1 lb potatoes, halved
salt and pepper
50 g / 2 oz butter
150 ml / ¼ pint fromage frais
8-12 large scallops, shelled, with corals
1 small onion, sliced
1 bay leaf
45 ml / 3 tbsp dry white wine
juice of ½ lemon
25 g / 1 oz plain flour
125 ml / 4 fl oz milk
45 ml / 3 tbsp dried white breadcrumbs
60 ml / 4 tbsp grated Parmesan cheese
watercress sprigs to garnish

Cook the potatoes in a saucepan of salted boiling water for about 30 minutes or until tender. Drain thoroughly and mash with a potato masher, or beat with a hand-held electric whisk until smooth. Beat in 25 g / 1 oz of the butter and 15 ml / 1 tbsp of the fromage frais to make a creamy piping consistency.

Grease 4 scallop shells or shallow individual ovenproof dishes. Spoon the creamed potato into a piping bag fitted with a large star nozzle and pipe a border of mashed potato around the edge of each shell. Set the oven at 200°C / 400°F / gas 6.

Combine the scallops, onion, bay leaf, wine and lemon juice in a saucepan. Add 75 ml / 5 tbsp water. Bring to simmering point and poach the scallops gently for 5 minutes. Using a slotted spoon, remove the scallops and cut into slices. Strain the cooking liquid into a jug.

Melt the remaining butter in a saucepan, add the flour and cook for 1 minute, stirring constantly. Gradually add the reserved cooking liquid, stirring all the time, until the sauce starts to thicken. Add salt and pepper to taste and stir in the milk. Bring to the boil, stirring, then lower the heat and simmer for 2-3 minutes. Remove from the heat and stir in the remaining fromage frais.

Divide the sliced scallops between the prepared scallop shells or dishes. Coat with the sauce and sprinkle lightly with the breadcrumbs and Parmesan.

Stand the scallop shells or dishes on a large baking sheet and bake for 10 minutes until the breadcrumbs are crisp and the potatoes browned. Garnish with the watercress sprigs and serve.

SERVES 4

Chicken Ramekins

FOOD VALUES	TOTAL	PER PORTION (4)
Protein	58g	15g
Carbohydrate	3g	1g
Fat	19g	5g
Fibre	1g	–
kcals	412	103

oil for greasing
175 g / 6 oz raw chicken or
    turkey meat, minced
2 eggs, separated
50 g / 2 oz mushrooms,
    chopped
salt and pepper
45 ml / 3 tbsp fromage frais
milk (see method)

Grease eight small ramekins. Set the oven at 190°C / 375°F / gas 5. Put the minced chicken or turkey in a bowl and gradually add the egg yolks, stirring to make a very smooth mixture. Stir in the mushrooms and set aside.

Whisk the egg whites with salt and pepper to taste in a clean, dry bowl until very stiff. Fold the fromage frais into the chicken mixture, then fold in the whisked egg whites. If the mixture is very stiff, add a little milk.

Divide the mixture between the prepared ramekins. Bake for about 30 minutes or until well risen, firm to the touch and browned. Serve at once.

SERVES 4 TO 8

Hot Chicken Liver Mousses

FOOD VALUES	TOTAL	PER PORTION
Protein	64g	16g
Carbohydrate	28g	7g
Fat	45g	11g
Fibre	1g	—
kcals	784	196

oil for greasing
15 ml / 1 tbsp butter
30 ml / 2 tbsp plain flour
150 ml / ¼ pint milk
salt and pepper
225 g / 8 oz chicken livers, trimmed
1 egg, plus 1 yolk
5 ml / 1 tsp Worcestershire sauce
45 ml / 3 tbsp fromage frais
15 ml / 1 tbsp dry sherry
30 ml / 2 tbsp snipped chives

Grease four 150 ml / ¼ pint ovenproof dishes. Set the oven at 180°C / 350°F / gas 4. Combine the butter, flour and milk in a small saucepan. Whisk over moderate heat until the mixture comes to the boil. Lower the heat and simmer for 3-4 minutes, whisking constantly, until the sauce is thick, smooth and glossy. Add salt and pepper to taste. Cover the surface with buttered greaseproof paper and cool.

Purée the livers in a blender or food processor or put them through a mincer twice. Scrape the purée into a bowl and beat in the egg and egg yolk. Add the Worcestershire sauce, fromage frais and dry sherry; stir in the sauce and chives.

Divide the liver mixture between the prepared dishes, place them in a deep baking tin and pour in enough boiling water to come halfway up the sides of the dishes. Bake for 25-30 minutes until a fine skewer inserted in the centre of one of the mousses comes out clean. Remove from the water and stand for 2-3 minutes before serving.

SERVES 4

Sherried Mushrooms

FOOD VALUES	TOTAL	PER PORTION (4)
Protein	17g	4g
Carbohydrate	31g	8g
Fat	33g	8g
Fibre	4g	1g
kcals	532	133

25 g / 1 oz butter
30 ml / 2 tbsp plain flour
250 ml / 8 fl oz milk
45 ml / 3 tbsp dry sherry
350 g / 12 oz mushrooms,
  sliced
salt and pepper
toast triangles to serve

Melt the butter in a saucepan, add the flour and cook for 1 minute. Gradually add the milk, stirring all the time until the mixture boils and thickens.

Stir in the sherry, then add the mushrooms, with salt and pepper to taste. Cook over gentle heat, stirring frequently, for about 5 minutes or until the mushrooms are just cooked.

Spoon on to a heated serving dish and serve at once, with toast triangles.

SERVES 4 TO 6

Mushrooms with Bacon and Wine

FOOD VALUES	TOTAL	PER PORTION
Protein	33g	6g
Carbohydrate	10g	2g
Fat	74g	12g
Fibre	5g	1g
kcals	879	147

6 rindless bacon rashers, chopped
400 g / 14 oz button mushrooms, halved or quartered if large
5 ml / 1 tsp snipped chives
5 ml / 1 tsp chopped parsley
10 ml / 2 tsp plain flour
75 ml / 5 tbsp white wine or cider
salt and pepper

Cook the bacon gently in a heavy-bottomed saucepan until the fat begins to run, then increase the heat to moderate and fry for 10 minutes. Add the mushrooms and herbs, tossing them in the bacon fat.

Sprinkle the flour over the mushrooms, cook for 1 minute, stirring gently, then add the wine or cider. Simmer for 10 minutes, stirring occasionally. Season and serve.

SERVES 6

MRS BEETON'S TIP

Store mushrooms in a paper bag inside a polythene bag. The paper absorbs condensation which helps to ensure that the mushrooms will keep for three days in the refrigerator.

Kipper and Tomato Bake

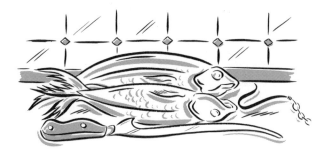

FOOD VALUES	TOTAL	PER PORTION
Protein	139g	35g
Carbohydrate	28g	7g
Fat	69g	17g
Fibre	2g	1g
kcals	1283	321

oil for greasing
250 ml / 8 fl oz milk
4 kippers
45 ml / 3 tbsp chopped
    parsley
15 ml / 1 tbsp fresh white
    breadcrumbs
lemon juice
salt and pepper
225 g / 8 oz tomatoes, sliced
chopped parsley to garnish

Grease a shallow ovenproof dish. Set the oven at 160°C / 325°F / gas 3. Heat the milk in a large frying pan, add the kippers and poach over gentle heat for 3 minutes. Remove the pan from the heat, cover and leave to stand for 5 minutes. Remove the kippers from the pan, reserving 30 ml / 2 tbsp of the poaching liquid. Skin and bone the kippers and flake the flesh.

In a bowl, mix the flaked kippers, the reserved poaching liquid, parsley and breadcrumbs. Add a little lemon juice and salt and pepper to taste.

Spread the mixture in the prepared dish, top with tomato slices and bake for 20 minutes. Sprinkle with chopped parsley before serving.

SERVES 4

MRS BEETON'S TIP

Try to find oak smoked kippers. The flavour is infinitely better than that of kippers which have been artificially dyed to an unnatural dark brown.

Saucy Angels

FOOD VALUES	TOTAL	PER PORTION
Protein	186g	16g
Carbohydrate	121g	10g
Fat	171g	14g
Fibre	4g	–
kcals	2734	228

6 rindless bacon rashers
5 ml / 1 tsp finely chopped
   onion
2.5 ml / ½ tsp chopped
   parsley
125 ml / 4 fl oz thick white
   sauce, see Mrs Beeton's
   Tip
2.5 ml / ½ tsp lemon juice
paprika
salt
800 g / 1¾ lb canned or
   bottled mussels, drained
12 small rounds of toast

Set the oven at 180°C / 350°F / gas 4. Using a rolling pin, stretch and flatten each rasher of bacon. Cut them in half. Stir the onion and parsley into the white sauce, add the lemon juice and season with paprika and a little salt. Stir in the mussels.

Spoon 2 or 3 mussels with sauce on to each piece of bacon. Roll up carefully, securing each bacon roll with a small skewer. Place on a baking sheet and bake for 7-8 minutes. Serve hot on toast.

MAKES 12

MRS BEETON'S TIP

It is not practical to make white sauce in very small quantities. The recipe that follows yields 300 ml / ½ pint of a thick sauce, suitable for coating: Melt 25 g / 1oz butter in a saucepan, stir in 25 g / 1 oz plain flour and cook over low heat for 2-3 minutes without browning. Gradually add 300 ml / ½ pint milk, stirring constantly until the sauce boils and thickens. Simmer for 1-2 minutes, beating briskly. Use 125 ml / 4 fl oz of the sauce in the recipe above; cover the rest with dampened greaseproof paper and refrigerate for use in another recipe.

Angels on Horseback

FOOD VALUES	TOTAL	PER PORTION
Protein	97g	12g
Carbohydrate	49g	6g
Fat	221g	28g
Fibre	2g	–
kcals	2557	320

8 *large shelled oysters*
8 *rindless bacon rashers*
2-3 *slices of bread*
butter for spreading

Wrap each oyster in a bacon rasher. Fasten the rolls with small poultry skewers, place in a grill pan and grill for 4-6 minutes.

Meanwhile toast the bread. Spread with butter and cut into small fingers. Remove the skewers from the bacon rolls and serve on toast fingers.

MAKES 8

NUTRITION NOTE

Oysters provide calcium; however, the most important supply is milk and milk products and fish which are eaten with their bones, such as canned sardines. Traditionally, canned salmon has always been thought of as a valuable source of calcium; however, this depends on whether the comparatively soft bones are crushed and consumed with the fish. The importance of mashing the bones with the fish was emphasized in wartime cooking advice, when citizens were presented with the best ways of maximizing the nutrient content of rationed foods. These days it is questionable whether many people would actually take that advice and mash the bones with the salmon flesh as doing so does not make a positive contribution to the flavour and texture of the fish.

THE SAVOURY

Savouries were, in Mrs Beeton's day, served at the end of the meal, after the dessert, in the same way as the French served cheese – but the savoury was very much a feature of the British dinner party menu.

Angels on Horseback (page 103) is a classic example of a savoury, and one of the lighter options. Rich dishes of melted cheese – fondue-like creations, often further enriched with butter – would frequently be presented on spirit burners to tempt those who were not already filled to satisfaction.

They were, of course, the perfect palate-preparation for port and many people who do not have a particularly sweet tooth still like to end the meal on a savoury note.

Serving a savoury is a good idea if you want to provide diners with an alternative to a rich dessert – or a rich cheese course, for that matter. In the context of planning lighter menus, some of the spreads suggested for toast toppers (page 120) are ideal candidates for the savoury course. Here are a few additional suggestions.

SIMPLE HOT SAVOURIES

The following are ideal for serving on toast or on warm Bath Oliver or water biscuits.

- Steamed asparagus tips, topped with a few thin slivers of Gruyère cheese and lightly toasted.
- Sliced green olives topped with a few strips of cooked ham and a little diced mozzarella.
- Chopped smoked salmon with a little dill and fromage frais.
- Thinly sliced artichoke bottoms, topped with low-fat soft cheese and chives.
- Thin slices of pear topped with blue Stilton cheese.

FINGER SAVOURIES

- Scallops wrapped in cooked ham and grilled.
- Button mushrooms, quickly sautéed in butter and rolled in chopped parsley and browned breadcrumbs.
- Ready-to-eat dried apricots filled with low-fat soft cheese.
- Walnut halves sandwiched with soft cheese and chives.
- Fresh dates filled with slivers of goats' milk cheese.
- Cubes of feta cheese served with quartered fresh figs.

SUPPERS AND SNACKS

Lentil and Broccoli Gratin

FOOD VALUES	TOTAL	PER PORTION (4)
Protein	132g	33g
Carbohydrate	153g	38g
Fat	110g	27g
Fibre	38g	10g
kcals	2140	535

225 g / 8 oz green or brown lentils

2 onions, chopped

1 bay leaf

750 ml / 1 ¼ pints Vegetable Stock (page 20)

450 g / 1 lb broccoli, broken into small florets

30 ml / 2 tbsp oil

6 tomatoes, peeled and quartered

150 ml / ¼ pint medium cider

salt and pepper

225 g / 8 oz mozzarella cheese, diced

Place the lentils in a saucepan with half the chopped onion, the bay leaf and the stock. Bring to the boil, then lower the heat and cover the pan. Simmer the lentils for 40-50 minutes, until they are tender and most of the stock has been absorbed. Check that they do not become dry during cooking. Replace the cover, remove from the heat and leave to stand.

Meanwhile, cook the broccoli in a saucepan of boiling water for 2-3 minutes, until just tender. Drain. Heat the oil in a large flameproof casserole and add the remaining onion. Cook, stirring, for 10-15 minutes, or until softened. Stir in the broccoli, tomatoes and cider with salt and pepper. Cook, stirring occasionally, for 15 minutes.

Discard the bay leaf from the lentils, then tip them into the pan with the broccoli mixture. Stir to combine all the ingredients. Taste and add more salt and pepper if required. Top with the mozzarella cheese and grill until the cheese is bubbling, crisp and golden. Serve piping hot.

SERVES 4 TO 6

Tofu and Spring Onion Stir Fry

This tasty stir fry goes well with cooked rice or Oriental noodles.

FOOD VALUES	TOTAL	PER PORTION
Protein	38g	10g
Carbohydrate	27g	7g
Fat	51g	13g
Fibre	6g	2g
kcals	746	187

350 g / 12 oz firm tofu cut
　　into 2.5 cm / 1 inch cubes
1 garlic clove, crushed
45 ml / 3 tbsp soy sauce
5 cm / 2 inch fresh root
　　ginger, peeled and
　　chopped
5 ml / 1 tsp sesame oil
5 ml / 1 tsp cornflour
30 ml / 2 tbsp dry sherry
60 ml / 4 tbsp Vegetable
　　Stock (page 20)
30 ml / 2 tbsp oil
1 red pepper, seeded and
　　diced
1 bunch of spring onions,
　　trimmed and sliced
　　diagonally
100 g / 4 oz button
　　mushrooms, sliced
salt and pepper

Place the tofu in a large, shallow dish. Mix the garlic, soy sauce, ginger and sesame oil in a bowl, then sprinkle the mixture evenly over the tofu. Cover and leave to marinate for 1 hour. In a jug, blend the cornflour to a paste with the sherry, then stir in the stock and set aside.

Heat the oil in a wok or large frying pan. Add the tofu and stir fry until lightly browned. Add the red pepper and continue cooking for 2-3 minutes before stirring in the spring onions. Once the onions are combined with the tofu, make a space in the middle of the pan and stir fry the mushrooms for 2 minutes.

Pour in the cornflour mixture and stir all the ingredients together. Bring the juices to the boil, stirring all the time, then lower the heat and simmer for 2 minutes. Taste the mixture for seasoning, then serve.

SERVES 4

NUTRITION NOTE

Tofu, or bean curd as it is also known, is made from ground soya beans. It is a protein-rich food, providing protein of comparable quality to that derived from animal sources, and it has a low fat content.

Corn Pudding

FOOD VALUES	TOTAL	PER PORTION
Protein	54g	9g
Carbohydrate	211g	35g
Fat	41g	7g
Fibre	9g	2g
kcals	1368	228

oil for greasing
100 g / 4 oz plain flour
5 ml / 1 tsp salt
2.5 ml / ½ tsp black pepper
2 eggs, beaten
500 ml / 17 fl oz milk
*400 g / 14 oz fresh or frozen
    sweetcorn kernels*

Grease a 1.5 litre / 2¾ pint pie or ovenproof dish.
Set the oven at 180°C / 350°F / gas 4. Sift the flour,
salt and pepper into a bowl. Add the beaten eggs,
stirring well. Beat in the milk to form a batter. Stir in
the corn. Turn into the prepared dish. Bake for
1 hour. Serve.

SERVES 6

NUTRITION NOTE

Corn pudding is a good example of a carbohydrate-rich dish with a
comparatively low fat content. Serve it with a substantial side salad of thinly
sliced peppers, lightly cooked French beans and tomatoes on a spinach base
to make a well-balanced supper dish.

Cornish Pasties

One Cornish pasty per person makes a hearty snack or a satisfying lunch when served with a generous portion of mixed salad. You may wish to use half wholemeal flour in the pastry to contribute additional fibre to the pasties.

FOOD VALUES	TOTAL	PER PORTION
Protein	117g	15g
Carbohydrate	466g	58g
Fat	231g	28g
Fibre	24g	3g
kcals	4298	537

PASTRY
500 g / 18 oz plain flour
5 ml / 1 tsp salt
150 g / 5 oz lard
60 ml / 4 tbsp shredded suet
flour for rolling out
beaten egg for glazing

FILLING
1 large or 2 small potatoes
1 small turnip
1 onion, chopped
salt and pepper
300 g / 11 oz lean chuck
    steak, finely diced

Set the oven at 230°C / 450°F / gas 8. To make the pastry, sift the flour and salt into a bowl. Rub in the lard, then mix in the suet. Moisten with enough cold water to make a stiff dough. Roll out on a lightly floured surface and cut into eight 16 cm / 6½ inch rounds.

To make the filling, dice the potatoes and turnip, then mix with the onion and add salt and pepper to taste. Add the meat and 30 ml / 2 tbsp water, and mix well. Divide between the pastry rounds, placing a line of mixture across the centre of each round.

Dampen the edges of each pastry round. Lift them to meet over the filling. Pinch together to seal, then flute the edges. Make small slits in both sides of each pasty near the top. Place the pasties on a baking sheet and brush with egg. Bake for 10 minutes, then lower the oven temperature to 180°C / 350°F / gas 4. Continue baking for a further 45 minutes, or until the meat is tender when pierced by a thin, heated skewer through the top of a pasty.

MAKES 8

Quiche Lorraine

A large quiche is ideal for cutting into small portions to serve as a light snack but you may prefer to make individual quiches to serve as a satisfying starter. Individual quiche dishes measure about 10 cm / 4 inches in diameter.

FOOD VALUES	TOTAL	PER PORTION
Protein	75g	13g
Carbohydrate	94g	16g
Fat	187g	31g
Fibre	3g	1g
kcals	2333	389

225 g / 8 oz rindless bacon
   rashers
3 eggs
300 ml / ½ pint milk
2.5 ml / ½ tsp salt
grinding of black pepper
pinch of grated nutmeg
25 g / 1 oz butter, diced

SHORT CRUST PASTRY
100 g / 4 oz plain flour
2.5 ml / ½ tsp salt
50 g / 2 oz margarine (or
   half butter, half lard)
flour for rolling out

Set the oven at 200°C / 400°F / gas 6. To make the pastry, sift the flour and salt into a bowl, then rub in the margarine until the mixture resembles fine breadcrumbs. Add enough cold water to make a stiff dough. Press the dough together.

Roll out the pastry on a lightly floured surface and use to line an 18 cm / 7 inch flan tin or ring placed on a baking sheet. Line the pastry with greaseproof paper and fill with baking beans. Bake 'blind' for 20 minutes until the rim of the pastry is slightly browned but the base still soft. Remove the paper and beans. Reduce the oven temperature to 190°C / 375°F / gas 5.

Cut the bacon in 2 cm × 5mm / ¾ × ¼ inch strips. Dry fry for a few minutes. Drain and scatter the strips over the pastry base. Press in lightly. Beat the eggs, milk, salt, pepper and nutmeg. Pour the mixture into the pastry case and dot with butter. Bake for 30 minutes. Serve at once.

SERVES 6

Eggs in Cocottes

This light supper dish also makes an excellent starter, particularly when mushrooms or spinach are added as described in the variations.

FOOD VALUES	TOTAL	PER PORTION
Protein	32g	8g
Carbohydrate	3g	1g
Fat	49g	12g
Fibre	—	—
kcals	581	145

25 g / 1 oz butter
4 eggs
salt and pepper
60 ml / 4 tbsp milk

Butter 4 ramekins or cocottes at least 3.5cm / 1½ inches deep, and stand them in a baking tin containing enough warm water to come halfway up their sides. Set the oven at 180°C / 350°F / gas 4.

Break an egg into each warm dish and add salt and pepper to taste. Top with any remaining butter, cut into flakes. Spoon 15 ml / 1 tbsp milk over each egg.

Bake for 6-10 minutes, depending on the thickness of the dishes. The whites of the eggs should be just set. Wipe the outsides of the dishes and serve.

SERVES 4

VARIATIONS

- Shake ground nutmeg or cayenne pepper over the eggs before cooking.
- Sprinkle the eggs with very finely grated cheese before cooking.
- Put sliced, fried mushrooms, chopped ham, cooked diced chicken or lightly sautéed, diced Italian sausage in the bottom of each dish before adding the eggs.
- Put 15-30 ml / 1-2 tbsp spinach purée in the dishes before adding the eggs.

Moulded Eggs

FOOD VALUES	TOTAL	PER PORTION
Protein	45g	11g
Carbohydrate	67g	17g
Fat	71g	18g
Fibre	9g	2g
kcals	1025	266

50 g / 2 oz butter
30 ml / 2 tbsp finely chopped parsley
4 eggs
4 slices of wholemeal bread

Butter four dariole moulds generously, reserving the remaining butter. Set the oven at 180°C / 350°F / gas 4.

Coat the insides of the moulds lightly with the parsley. Break an egg into each, then put them in a baking tin. Pour in enough warm water to come halfway up the sides of the moulds. Bake for 10-12 minutes, until the egg whites are just firm.

Meanwhile, cut a circle 7.5 cm / 3 inches in diameter from each slice of bread. Toast the bread rounds until golden brown on each side, then spread with the remaining butter. Loosen the cooked eggs in the moulds, turn out on to the toast, and serve immediately.

SERVES 4

VARIATIONS

- About 15 ml / 1 tbsp finely snipped chives can be used instead of the parsley.
- Use 25 g / 1 oz mushrooms, finely chopped, cooked in butter and drained, instead of the parsley.
- Use 25 g / 1 oz minced ham mixed with 10 ml / 2 tsp chopped parsley instead of the parsley alone.
- Large flat mushrooms, lightly sautéed or grilled, can be used instead of the toast.
- Large (Beefsteak) tomatoes, peeled, cut in half and seeded, can be used instead of the toast.

Shirred Eggs

FOOD VALUES	TOTAL	PER PORTION
Protein	30g	8g
Carbohydrate	–	–
Fat	38g	10g
Fibre	–	–
kcals	463	116

butter for greasing
4 eggs
salt
1.25 ml / ¼ tsp paprika
10 ml / 2 tsp snipped chives
  or chopped parsley

Grease a shallow ovenproof dish, about 30 cm / 12 inches across. Set the oven at 180°C / 350°F / gas 4. Separate the eggs, keeping each yolk intact and separate.

Put the egg whites into a clean, dry bowl. Add 2.5 ml / ½ tsp salt and whisk to very stiff peaks. Spread the whites lightly over the prepared dish to form a layer about 5 cm / 2 inches deep.

Using the back of a spoon, make 4 hollows in the egg white. Space the hollows as evenly as possible and do not make them too near the edge. Slip 1 egg yolk into each hollow.

Bake for about 10 minutes or until the eggs are just set. Sprinkle with paprika and chives, or parsley and serve at once.

SERVES 4

VARIATION

Shirred Eggs on Toast Use four egg yolks but only two whites. Whisk the whites with 1.25 ml / ¼ tsp salt until very stiff and fold in 50 g / 2 oz finely grated Cheddar cheese. Lightly toast 4 slices of bread. Pile the cheesy meringue mixture on the toast, make a depression in each and slip in an egg yolk. Sprinkle about 15 ml / 1 tbsp grated cheese over each egg yolk and cook under a low grill until the meringue is golden and the egg yolks are cooked. Serve.

Framed Eggs

FOOD VALUES	TOTAL	PER PORTION
Protein	45g	11g
Carbohydrate	89g	22g
Fat	39g	10g
Fibre	3g	1g
kcals	866	217

4 thick slices of white bread
oil for shallow frying
4 eggs

Cut each slice of bread into a 10 cm / 4 inch round, then cut a second 6 cm / 2½ inch round from the centres, so that four bread rings are left.

Heat the oil in a large frying pan and fry the bread rings until brown and crisp on one side. Turn them over, lower the heat and break an egg into the centre of each ring. Fry gently, spooning the oil over the top from time to time, until the eggs are set. Using a fish slice, remove the framed eggs from the pan, draining excess oil, and serve at once.

SERVES 4

NUTRITION NOTE

Framed eggs are a sophisticated version of fried eggs, kept neat by the fried bread surround. Obviously, they are not an everyday dish. The fat content varies according to how much oil is used and absorbed in cooking. Use a thin coating of oil and ensure it is well heated before adding the bread so that the surface of the bread is quickly sealed. They are a good idea for a special-occasion fried breakfast or brunch.

Eggs Florentine

FOOD VALUES	TOTAL	PER PORTION
Protein	84g	21g
Carbohydrate	16g	4g
Fat	81g	20g
Fibre	21g	5g
kcals	1125	281

butter for greasing
1 kg / 2¼ lb fresh spinach
or 2 (225 g / 8 oz)
packets frozen leaf spinach
15 ml / 1 tbsp butter
salt and pepper
4 eggs
100 g / 4 oz Fontina or
Cheddar cheese, finely
grated

Set the oven at 190°C / 375°F / gas 5. Wash the fresh spinach several times and remove any coarse stalks. Put into a saucepan with just the water that clings to the leaves, then cover the pan with a tight-fitting lid. Place over moderate heat for about 3 minutes, shaking the pan often until the spinach has wilted. Lower the heat slightly and cook for 3-5 minutes more. (Cook frozen spinach according to the directions on the packet.)

When the spinach is tender, drain it thoroughly in a colander. Cut through the leaves several times with a knife to chop them roughly. Melt the butter in the clean pan, add the spinach with salt and pepper to taste, and heat through gently.

Spoon into a greased ovenproof dish and, using the back of a spoon, make 4 small hollows in the surface. Break an egg into each hollow, add salt and pepper to taste, then sprinkle the grated cheese over the eggs. Bake for 12-15 minutes until the eggs are lightly set. Serve at once.

SERVES 4

Eggs au Maître d'Hôtel

FOOD VALUES	TOTAL	PER PORTION
Protein	58g	15g
Carbohydrate	32g	8g
Fat	72g	18g
Fibre	1g	–
kcals	1001	250

25 g / 1 oz butter
30 ml / 2 tbsp plain flour
300 ml / ½ pint milk
salt and pepper
30 ml / 2 tbsp chopped
   parsley
6 eggs, hard boiled and
   quartered
juice of ½ lemon

Melt the butter in a small saucepan. Stir in the flour and cook for a few seconds, then gradually pour in the milk, stirring all the time. Bring to the boil, stirring, reduce the heat and leave the sauce to simmer gently for 5 minutes. Add the seasoning and parsley, and remove from the heat.

Arrange the eggs in a dish or in four individual dishes. Stir the lemon juice into the sauce, pour it over the eggs and serve.

SERVES 4

Oeufs au Plat

FOOD VALUES	TOTAL	PER PORTION
Protein	30g	8g
Carbohydrate	–	–
Fat	46g	12g
Fibre	–	–
kcals	537	134

25 g / 1 oz butter
4 eggs
salt and white pepper

Set the oven at 180°C / 350°F / gas 4 or heat the grill. Butter a shallow ovenproof or flameproof dish (for grilling). The lid of an ovenproof glass casserole or a medium quiche dish will do instead of a gratin dish.

Break the eggs into the dish and sprinkle with salt and white pepper. Dot with the remaining butter.

Bake for about 12 minutes, or until the eggs are cooked to taste. Alternatively, place them under the grill on a low rack. Cook for about 5 minutes, or until the eggs are set.

SERVES 4

Anchovy Eggs

FOOD VALUES	TOTAL	PER PORTION
Protein	43g	11g
Carbohydrate	59g	15g
Fat	92g	23g
Fibre	2g	1g
kcals	1219	305

4 *slices of white bread*
75 *g / 3 oz butter*
anchovy paste or essence
  (*see method*)
4 *eggs*
10 *ml / 2 tsp tarragon*
  vinegar
20 *ml / 4 tsp chopped*
  parsley

Toast the bread on both sides and cut off the crusts. Spread each slice with butter and a little anchovy paste or essence.

Melt the remaining butter in a frying pan and fry the eggs until set. Using a fish slice, transfer each egg to a slice of toast and keep hot.

Add the vinegar to the butter remaining in the frying pan. Heat until the mixture browns. Pour it over the eggs, top with the parsley and serve.

SERVES 4

Fish Custard

FOOD VALUES	TOTAL	PER PORTION
Protein	128g	32g
Carbohydrate	26g	7g
Fat	57g	14g
Fibre	–	–
kcals	1125	281

oil for greasing
450 g / 1 lb sole or plaice
    fillets, skinned
500 ml / 17 fl oz milk
4 eggs
grated rind of ½ lemon
30 ml / 2 tbsp chopped
    parsley
salt and pepper

Grease an ovenproof dish. Set the oven at 150°C / 300°F / gas 2. Arrange the fish fillets on the base of the dish.

Warm the milk in a saucepan, but do not allow it to approach boiling point. Beat the eggs, lemon rind, parsley, salt and pepper in a large bowl. Stir in the milk. Strain the custard over the fish in the dish.

Stand the dish in a roasting tin. Pour in enough boiling water to come halfway up the sides of the dish. Bake for 1½ hours or until the custard is set in the centre.

SERVES 4

VARIATION

Smoked Cod Custard Bring the milk to simmering point in a saucepan, add 450 g / 1 lb smoked cod and poach for 10 minutes. Drain, reserving the milk in a measuring jug. Remove any skin or bones from the fish and flake the flesh into the prepared dish. Make up the milk to 500 ml / 17 fl oz if necessary. Use the warm (not hot) fish-flavoured milk to make the custard. Proceed as above.

Cheese and Asparagus Custard

It is desirable to cook asparagus upright, so that the stalks are poached while the delicate tips are gently steamed. If the asparagus is too tall for the saucepan, cover it with a dome of foil, crumpled around the pan's rim, instead of using the lid. You can buy asparagus pans from specialist kitchen shops.

FOOD VALUES	TOTAL	PER PORTION
Protein	81g	20g
Carbohydrate	30g	8g
Fat	84g	21g
Fibre	3g	1g
kcals	1186	297

butter for greasing
1 bundle of small or sprue asparagus, trimmed or 225 g / 8 oz canned or frozen asparagus
100 g / 4 oz cheese, grated
4 eggs
salt and pepper
500 ml / 17 fl oz milk

Butter a 750ml / 1¼ pint ovenproof dish. Tie fresh asparagus in small bundles. Add enough salted water to a deep saucepan to come three-quarters of the way up the stalks. Bring to the boil. Wedge the bundles of asparagus upright in the pan, or stand them in a heatproof container in the pan. Cover and cook gently for about 10 minutes, depending on the thickness of the stalks. Drain carefully. Drain canned asparagus or cook frozen asparagus according to the directions on the packet.

Set the oven at 150°C / 300°F / gas 2. Cut the asparagus into short lengths and put it into the prepared dish, with the tips arranged on the top. Sprinkle the grated cheese over the asparagus. Beat the eggs, salt and pepper together lightly and stir in the milk. Strain the custard into the dish.

Stand the dish in a shallow tin containing enough warm water to come halfway up the sides of the dish. Bake for 1½ hours, until the custard is set in the centre.

SERVES 4

TASTY TOPPERS

Toast toppers will always be a favourite snack and many are easily elevated to the position of the more elegant savoury (see page 104). Although they are always thought of as toppings to serve on toast, many are delicious on toasted muffins or crumpets, and they are ideal for serving on the exotic breads.

Spreads for Snacks or Savouries

- Mix finely chopped pitted black olives with a little olive oil, grated lemon rind and just enough soft cheese to bind the mixture to a paste. Spread on slim toast fingers or cocktail crackers.
- Make a piquant tomato spread by mixing tomato purée with olive oil, garlic, a little cayenne pepper and finely chopped spring onion. Spread thinly on plain cocktail crackers.
- Mash canned anchovy fillets to a paste, add a little low-fat soft cheese, grated lemon rind and freshly ground black pepper. Sharpen to taste with lemon juice and spread thinly on toast or thinly sliced rye bread.
- Pound smoked mackerel to a paste and soften with a little yogurt, then flavour with snipped chives. Spread on soft finger rolls or Melba toast.
- Mix finely chopped cooked ham with curd cheese. Season with a little paprika and finely chopped gherkin. Spread on slim Swedish-style rye crackers or fingers of toasted light rye bread.

Tasty Everyday Toast Toppers

- Mashed canned sardines, sharpened with lemon juice and seasoned with freshly ground black pepper. Spread on toast, toasted muffins or pitta bread and grill until hot.
- Mash drained canned tuna with a little grated cheese, chopped onion and tomato. Spread on toast, toasted crumpets or muffins and grill until golden.
- Top toast, warm pitta or naan with sliced tomatoes and chopped spring onion. Season well and trickle a little olive oil over, then grill until hot.
- Mix chopped button mushrooms with low-fat soft cheese and a little crumbled blue cheese. Spread on toast, crumpets or toasted muffins and grill until brown.

Substantial Toppings

- Poached eggs – delicious on toast, toasted muffins or crumpets.
- Crumpet Cordon Bleu – top a lightly toasted crumpet with a folded slice of ham and a slice of cheese. Grill until golden.
- Top crumpets or muffins with a whole open cup mushroom and bacon, then grill slowly until the bacon is crisp and the mushroom cooked.
- Grilled tomatoes are the ideal topping for thick slices of bread, large naan bread or pitta. Cut the tomatoes into quarters and arrange them on the bread base. Season well and sprinkle with a little cheese if liked, then grill until hot.

Lancashire Cheese and Onions

FOOD VALUES	TOTAL	PER PORTION
Protein	47g	12g
Carbohydrate	52g	13g
Fat	66g	16g
Fibre	8g	2g
kcals	974	244

5 large onions, thickly sliced
125 ml / 4 fl oz milk
salt and pepper
150 g / 5 oz Lancashire
   cheese, grated or crumbled
15 ml / 1 tbsp butter
hot buttered toast to serve

Put the onions in a saucepan with water to cover. Boil for 20-25 minutes, or until the onions are tender and the water has almost evaporated. Add the milk, with salt and pepper to taste, and bring to the boil again.

Remove from the heat and add the grated or crumbled cheese. Stir in the butter. Leave to stand for 7-10 minutes or until the cheese has fully melted. Stir once; reheat without boiling. Serve immediately, with hot lightly buttered wholemeal toast.

SERVES 4

MRS BEETON'S TIP

Lancashire Cheese and Onions is a delicious filling for fluffy baked potatoes. Do not put any butter into the potatoes – it is quite unnecessary since the cheese and onions are sufficiently well flavoured.

Mrs Beeton's Baked Cheese Sandwiches

FOOD VALUES	TOTAL	PER PORTION
Protein	55g	14g
Carbohydrate	173g	43g
Fat	73g	18g
Fibre	5g	1g
kcals	1529	382

8 *slices of bread*
butter
4 *large thick slices of*
Cheshire or Cheddar
cheese

Set the oven at 200°C / 400°F / gas 6 and heat a baking sheet. Spread the bread with the butter and make 4 cheese sandwiches.

Spread the top of each sandwich very lightly with butter, then invert them on the hot baking sheet. Spread the top of each sandwich very lightly with butter. Bake for 5 minutes, turn the sandwiches and bake for a further 5 minutes, until golden. Serve.

SERVES 4

NUTRITION NOTE

Although butter would have been spread on the bread traditionally, there is no need to use it in the sandwiches if you want to reduce their overall fat content. The cheese will yield sufficient fat during cooking to moisten the bread. If you make the sandwiches frequently, it is a good idea to use a full-flavoured reduced-fat hard cheese.

BREADS AND CRACKERS

BREAD AND CRACKER ACCOMPANIMENTS

Breads and crackers play an important role as accompaniments for first courses, bases for appetizers and savouries, and substantial fillers for hearty snacks. Bread, and particularly wholemeal varieties, is an essential feature of a well-balanced Western diet, providing minerals and vitamins as well as an extremely useful source of fibre. Perhaps a key mistake to avoid is always to spread fat (butter or margarine) on breads and crackers. It is a good idea to get into the habit of adopting a more Mediterranean approach by serving large chunks of bread to mop cooking juices and to complement salads.

YEASTED BREADS

The aroma of freshly baked bread is unmistakable and appetizing, and the results are worth the effort. This chapter offers a wide selection of recipes, from plain white or wholemeal loaves to specialist International breads.

The choice of ingredients for making yeast mixtures is important. Strong flour is used because of its high gluten content. Gluten is the strengthening agent which forms the elastic dough during kneading, to trap the bubbles of gas given off by the yeast during proving. This makes the dough rise and gives the light result.

Yeast
There are various options and all work well.

Fresh yeast Available from bakers who cook on the premises, small bread shops, hot bread shops or the hot bread counters at larger supermarkets.

Fresh yeast should be pale, firm and slightly crumbly in texture. It should smell fresh. Yeast that is very broken, dark, soft or sour-smelling is old and should not be used. Wrapped in polythene, fresh yeast will keep for several days in the refrigerator or it may be frozen. Freeze 25 g / 1 oz portions ready for use.

Cream fresh yeast with a little sugar and lukewarm liquid to make a paste. Add a little extra liquid, then place the mixture in a warm place until it becomes frothy. This process gives the yeast a good start so that it is very active when mixed with the other ingredients. It is also a very good way of checking that the yeast is fresh and working.

There has been some controversy over whether the yeast should be creamed with sugar or just with water. The addition of sugar was thought to give an unacceptably strong 'yeasty' flavour to the finished baked goods but as long as the quantities in recipes are followed correctly, and the liquid is not left for too long, the results using sugar are better than without.

Other methods of starting the yeast include sponging it – mixing it to a paste, then adding all the liquid and enough flour to make a batter. This is left to rise and bubble before the ingredients are mixed to a dough. Sometimes the yeast liquid may be poured into a well in the dry ingredients and allowed to ferment, usually sprinkled with a little flour.

Dried yeasts There are two types, so always read the manufacturer's instructions and follow them carefully. The first is a granular product that is sprinkled over warm liquid and left to dissolve, then to ferment until frothy before being stirred and mixed with the remaining ingredients. Usually the granules contain enough food for the yeast to work without having to add extra sugar.

The second, newer and now more popular type is a finer-grained dried yeast which should be added to the dry ingredients. Slightly hotter liquid is used to mix the dough and only one rising, or proving, is necessary.

Techniques

Kneading The kneading is important as it mixes the yeast evenly with the other ingredients and develops the gluten in the flour to make the dough elastic. Once the dough is toughened, it traps the bubbles of gas produced by the yeast and rises.

Proving This is the process of rising. The dough must be left in a warm place until it has doubled in bulk. It must be covered to keep in moisture and to prevent a skin forming on the dough (polythene, cling film or a damp cloth may be used). The covering is removed after proving, before baking. The warmer the site, the faster the rising but if the dough becomes hot the yeast will be killed. Dough may be left overnight in the refrigerator to rise slowly, or in a cool place for many hours. In a warm room dough will rise in a couple of hours.

Except when using fast-action dried yeast (the type combined with dry ingredients), most doughs are proved twice.

Knocking Back After the first proving, the dough is very lightly kneaded to knock out the gas, then it is shaped and allowed to prove for a second time. The second kneading is known as knocking back.

Storing

Breads should be stored in a clean airtight container. If kept in a polythene bag, they should be placed in a cool place (but not the refrigerator which tends to promote staling) to prevent them from sweating.

Freezing

Yeasted goods freeze well – they should be cooked and cooled, then packed and frozen promptly. Most breads freeze well for up to 2 months. Loaves should be left to thaw for several hours at room temperature; rolls and small items thaw within a couple of hours at room temperature.

Basic White Bread

FOOD VALUES	TOTAL	PER 25g / 1 oz
Protein	95g	2g
Carbohydrates	608g	13g
Fat	36g	0.75g
Fibre	25g	0.5g
kcals	2984	61

oil for greasing
800 g / 1¾ lb strong white
flour
10 ml / 2 tsp salt
25 g / 1 oz lard
25 g / 1 oz fresh yeast or
15 ml / 1 tbsp dried yeast
2.5 ml / ½ tsp sugar
flour for kneading
beaten egg or milk for
glazing

Grease two 23 x 13 x 7.5 cm / 9 x 5 x 3 inch loaf tins. Sift the flour and salt into a large bowl. Rub in the lard. Measure 500 ml / 17 fl oz lukewarm water.

Blend the fresh yeast to a thin paste with the sugar and a little of the warm water. Set aside in a warm place until frothy – about 5 minutes. Alternatively, sprinkle dried yeast over all the warm water and set aside. When frothy, stir well.

Add the yeast liquid and remaining water to the flour mixture and mix to a soft dough. Turn on to a floured surface and knead for about 8 minutes or until the dough is smooth, elastic and no longer sticky. Return to the bowl and cover with cling film. Leave in a warm place until the dough has doubled in bulk – this will take up to 2 hours, or longer.

Knead the dough again until firm. Cut into two equal portions and form each into a loaf shape. Place the dough into the prepared loaf tins and

126

brush the surface of each with beaten egg or milk. Place the tins in a large, lightly oiled polythene bag. Leave in a warm place for about 45 minutes or until the dough has doubled in bulk. Set the oven at 230°C / 450°F / gas 8.

Bake for 35-40 minutes, until the loaves are crisp and golden brown, and sound hollow when tapped on the bottom.

MAKES TWO 800 G / 1¾ LB LOAVES

NUTRITION NOTE

Even though they are small, quantities for fat and fibre are included in the Basic White Bread and Rice Bread (page 130) recipes because the information may be useful when multiplying the portion size to reflect the amount of bread eaten during any one day or at a particular meal. Also, this provides a useful comparison with wholemeal recipes.

SHAPING YEAST DOUGH

Yeast doughs of all types may be shaped in many ways to make attractive breads. The following ideas may be used for making two loaves from the Basic White Bread dough recipe.

Twist Divide the dough in half and roll each piece into a strip. Pinch the two ends of the strips together on a greased baking sheet, then twist the strips together, tucking the ends under neatly and pinching them in place.

Ring Make a long, fairly slim twist, then shape it in a ring on a greased baking sheet.

Plait Divide the dough for one loaf into three equal portions and roll them into long strips. Pinch the ends of the strips together on a greased baking sheet, then plait the strips neatly. Fold the ends under at the end of the plait, pinching them underneath to secure the plait.

Cottage Loaf Shape two-thirds of the dough into a round loaf and place on a greased baking sheet. Shape the remaining dough into a ball. Make an indentation in the middle of the round loaf, then dampen the dough in the middle and place the ball on top. Make a deep indentation with your fingers or a wooden spoon handle down through the ball of dough and the round base. Before baking, score several slits down the side of the base of the loaf.

Toppings for Breads

Before baking, the risen dough may be glazed with beaten egg or milk for a golden crust. Brushing with water makes a crisp crust. Then the dough may be sprinkled with any of the following:

- Poppy seeds – dark or white.
- Sesame seeds – black or white, for flavour as well as texture and appearance.
- Cracked wheat – good on wholemeal loaves.
- Caraway, fennel or cumin seeds – when used generously these all contribute flavour.

Fancy Roll Shapes

Divide the risen Basic White Bread dough (page 126) into 50 / 2 oz pieces and shape as below:

Small Plaits Divide each piece of dough into three equal portions; then shape each of these into a long strand. Plait the three strands together, pinching the ends securely.

Small Twists Divide each piece of dough into two equal portions, and shape into strands about 12 cm / 4½ inches in length. Twist the two strands together, pinching the ends securely.

'S' Rolls Shape each piece of dough into a roll about 15 cm / 6 inches in length, and form it into an 'S' shape.

Cottage Rolls Cut two-thirds off each piece of dough and shape into a ball. Shape the remaining third in the same way. Place the small ball on top of the larger one and push a hole through the centre of both with one finger, dusted with flour, to join the two pieces firmly together.

MAKES 24

Dinner Rolls

FOOD VALUES	TOTAL	PER ROLL
Protein	117g	5g
Carbohydrate	632g	26g
Fat	76g	3g
Fibre	25g	1g
kcals	3523	147

oil for greasing
800 g / 1¾ lb strong white
　flour
10 ml / 2 tsp sugar
400 ml / 14 fl oz milk
25 g / 1 oz fresh yeast or
　15 ml / 1 tbsp dried yeast
10 ml / 2 tsp salt
50 g / 2 oz butter or
　margarine
1 egg
flour for kneading
beaten egg for glazing

Grease two baking sheets. Sift about 75 g / 3 oz of the flour and all the sugar into a large bowl. Warm the milk until lukewarm, then blend in the fresh yeast or stir in the dried yeast. Pour the yeast liquid into the flour and sugar and beat well. Leave the bowl in a warm place for 20 minutes.

Sift the remaining flour and the salt into a bowl. Rub in the butter or margarine. Beat the egg into the yeast mixture and stir in the flour mixture. Mix to a soft dough. Turn on to a lightly floured surface and knead for about 5 minutes or until the dough is smooth and no longer sticky. Return to the bowl and cover with cling film. Leave in a warm place until the dough has doubled in bulk – this will take up to 2 hours, or longer.

Knead the dough again until firm. Cut into 50 g / 2 oz pieces, then shape each piece into a ball. Place on the prepared baking sheets 5-7.5 cm / 2-3 inches apart. Brush with beaten egg. Cover with sheets of lightly oiled polythene. Leave in a warm place for about 20 minutes or until the rolls have doubled in bulk. Set the oven at 220°C / 425°F / gas 7.

Bake for 12-15 minutes until the rolls are golden brown.

MAKES 24

Rice Bread

This unusual bread is moist with a close, slightly elastic, texture. It is delicious thickly sliced when warm or cut into thin slices when cold.

FOOD VALUES	TOTAL	PER 25g / 1oz
Protein	78g	2g
Carbohydrate	451g	12g
Fat	29g	1g
Fibre	14g	0.5g
kcals	2267	59

*100 g / 4 oz long-grain rice
(not the easy-cook type)
450 ml / ¾ pint milk
25 g / 1 oz fresh yeast or
15 ml / 1 tbsp dried yeast
2.5 ml / ½ tsp sugar
450 g / 1 lb strong plain
flour
10 ml / 2 tsp salt
beaten egg to glaze
(optional)*

Add the rice to a small saucepan of boiling water. Bring back to the boil, then drain. Put the rice back in the pan and add the milk. Bring to the boil, stirring occasionally, then reduce the heat and partially cover the pan. Simmer for 15 minutes.

Blend the fresh yeast to a thin paste with the sugar and 50 ml / 2 fl oz lukewarm water. Set aside in a warm place until frothy – about 5 minutes. Alternatively, sprinkle dried yeast over the water, set aside until frothy, then stir well.

Mix the flour and salt in a bowl. Make a well in the middle and pour in the rice with the cooking milk. Mix in the flour, using a wooden spoon and a cutting action. When the rice and milk are evenly distributed and have cooled slightly, pour in the yeast liquid and mix to a soft dough. The flour should have cooled the rice sufficiently to avoid killing the yeast but the dough should still feel hot.

Turn out on a well-floured surface and knead until smooth and elastic, sprinkling with a little flour to prevent the dough sticking. Place in a bowl, cover and leave in a warm place until doubled in bulk. Meanwhile, grease a baking sheet.

Turn the dough out, knead briefly and divide it in half. Shape two long oval loaves and place them on the baking sheet. Cover loosely with oiled polythene and leave in a warm place until well risen and spread into slightly flattened loaves. Meanwhile, set the oven at 220°C / 425°F / gas 7. Brush the risen loaves with beaten egg and bake for 35-45 minutes, until well browned and firm. The loaves should sound hollow when tapped on the bottom. Cool on a wire rack.

MAKES 2 LOAVES

Grant Loaf

FOOD VALUES	TOTAL	PER 25g / 1oz
Protein	104g	4g
Carbohydrate	514g	17g
Fat	18g	0.5g
Fibre	72g	3g
kcals	2503	83

oil for greasing
800 g / 1¾ lb wholemeal
*   flour*
15 ml / 1 tbsp salt
25 g / 1 oz fresh yeast or
*   15 ml / 1 tbsp dried yeast*
2.5 ml / ½ tsp sugar

Grease three 20 x 10 x 6 cm / 8 x 4 x 2½ inch loaf tins. Mix the flour and salt in a large bowl. Have ready 700 ml / scant 1¼ pints lukewarm water.

Blend the fresh yeast to a thin paste with the sugar and a little of the warm water. Set aside in a warm place until frothy – about 5 minutes. Alternatively, sprinkle dried yeast over all the warm water, set aside until frothy, then stir well.

Pour the yeast liquid and any remaining water into the flour and stir until the flour is evenly wetted. The resulting dough should be wet and slippery. Spoon it into the prepared loaf tins. Place the tins in a large, lightly oiled polythene bag. Leave in a warm place until the dough has risen by a third. Set the oven at 190°C / 375°F / gas 5. Bake for 50-60 minutes, until the loaves are brown and crisp, and sound hollow when tapped on the bottom.

MAKES THREE 400 G / 14 OZ LOAVES

Malted Brown Bread

FOOD VALUES	TOTAL	PER 25g / 1oz
Protein	104g	4g
Carbohydrate	514g	17g
Fat	18g	0.5g
Fibre	72g	2g
kcals	2503	83

oil for greasing
800 g / 1¾ lb wholemeal
   flour
15 ml / 1 tbsp salt
25 g / 1 oz fresh yeast or
   15 ml / 1 tbsp dried yeast
2.5 ml / ½ tsp sugar
30 ml / 2 tbsp malt extract
flour for kneading

Grease two 23 x 13 x 7.5 cm / 9 x 5 x 3 inch loaf tins. Mix the flour and salt in a large bowl. Measure 500 ml / 17 floz lukewarm water.

Blend the fresh yeast to a thin paste with the sugar and a little of the warm water. Set aside in a warm place until frothy – about 5 minutes. Alternatively, sprinkle the dried yeast over all the warm water and set aside until frothy.

Stir the malt extract into the yeast liquid with any remaining water. Add to the flour and mix to a soft dough. Turn on to a lightly floured surface and knead for about 4 minutes or until the dough is smooth, elastic and no longer sticky. Return to the bowl and cover with cling film. Leave in a warm place until the dough has doubled in bulk – this takes 2 hours, or longer.

Knead the dough again until firm. Cut into two equal portions and form each into a loaf shape. Place the dough in the prepared loaf tins. Place the tins in a large, lightly oiled polythene bag. Leave in a warm place for about 45 minutes or until the dough has doubled in bulk. Set the oven at 230°C / 450°F / gas 8.

Bake for 35-45 minutes, until the loaves are golden brown and crisp, and sound hollow when tapped on the bottom.

MAKES TWO 800 G / 1¾ LB LOAVES

Scottish Brown Bread

FOOD VALUES	TOTAL	PER 25g / 1oz
Protein	98g	4g
Carbohydrate	502g	17g
Fat	31g	1g
Fibre	66g	2g
kcals	2556	88

oil for greasing
575 g / 1¼ lb wholemeal
*   flour*
200 g / 7 oz fine or medium
*   oatmeal*
15 ml / 1 tbsp salt
25 g / 1 oz fresh yeast or
*   15 ml / 1 tbsp dried yeast*
2.5 ml / ½ tsp sugar
5 ml / 1 tsp bicarbonate of
*   soda*
flour for kneading

Grease two 23 x 13 x 7.5 cm / 9 x 5 x 3 inch loaf tins. Mix the flour, oatmeal and salt in a large bowl. Measure 500 ml / 17 floz lukewarm water. Blend the fresh yeast to a thin paste with the sugar and a little of the warm water. Set aside in a warm place until frothy – about 5 minutes. Alternatively, sprinkle dried yeast over all the warm water and set aside until frothy, then stir.

Add the bicarbonate of soda to the yeast liquid, with any remaining water, then stir this into the flour mixture to form a soft dough. Turn on to a lightly floured surface and knead for about 4 minutes or until the dough is smooth and no longer sticky. Return to the bowl and cover with cling film. Leave in a warm place until doubled in bulk – this will take up to 2 hours, or longer.

Knead the dough again until firm. Cut into two equal portions and form each into a loaf shape. Place the dough in the prepared loaf tins. Place the tins in a large, lightly oiled polythene bag. Leave in a warm place for about 45 minutes or until the dough has doubled in bulk. Set the oven at 230°C / 450°F / gas 8.

Bake for 20 minutes, then reduce the oven temperature to 190°C / 375°F / gas 5. Bake for 25-35 minutes, until the loaves are crisp and brown, and sound hollow when tapped on the bottom.

MAKES TWO 800 G / 1¾ LB LOAVES

Rye Cobs

FOOD VALUES	TOTAL	PER 25g / 1oz
Protein	162g	2g
Carbohydrate	1100g	15g
Fat	82g	1g
Fibre	81g	1g
kcals	5513	74

oil for greasing
900 g / 2 lb strong white
*   flour*
25 g / 1 oz fresh yeast or
*   15 ml / 1 tbsp dried yeast*
2.5 ml / ½ tsp sugar
450 g / 1 lb coarse rye flour
500 ml / 17 fl oz skimmed
*   milk*
20 ml / 4 tsp salt
60 ml / 4 tbsp molasses
60 ml / 4 tbsp cooking oil
flour for kneading

Grease two baking sheets or four 15 cm / 6 inch sandwich tins. Sift the white flour into a large bowl. Measure 250 ml / 8 fl oz lukewarm water.

Blend the fresh yeast to a thin paste with the sugar and a little of the warm water. Set aside in a warm place until frothy – about 5 minutes. Alternatively, sprinkle dried yeast over all the warm water and set aside until frothy, then stir well.

Mix the rye flour into the white flour. Add the yeast liquid, any remaining water, the skimmed milk, salt, molasses and oil, then knead to a soft dough. Cover the bowl with cling film. Leave in a warm place until the dough has doubled in bulk – this will take at least 2 hours, or longer. (Rye bread is slow to rise).

When risen, shape into four loaves. Place on the prepared baking sheets or press into the sandwich tins. Place in a large, lightly oiled polythene bag. Leave to rise for 30-45 minutes. Set the oven at 190°C / 375°F / gas 5.

Sprinkle the dough with warm water. Bake for about 40 minutes, until the loaves sound hollow when tapped on the bottom.

MAKES 4 LOAVES

Challah

FOOD VALUES	TOTAL	PER PORTION
Protein	110g	3g
Carbohydrate	613g	16g
Fat	106g	–
Fibre	25g	0.75g
kcals	3694	97

oil for greasing
800 g / 1¾ lb strong white
*   flour*
10 ml / 2 tsp sugar
25 g / 1 oz fresh yeast or
*   15 ml / 1 tbsp dried yeast*
10 ml / 2 tsp salt
100 g / 4 oz butter or
*   margarine*
2 eggs
flour for kneading
beaten egg for glazing

Grease two baking sheets. Sift about 75 g / 3 oz of the flour and all the sugar into a large bowl. Measure 400 ml / 14 fl oz lukewarm water. Blend the fresh yeast into the water or stir in the dried yeast. Pour the yeast liquid into the flour and sugar and beat well. Leave in a warm place for 20 minutes.

Sift the remaining flour and the salt into a bowl. Rub in the butter or margarine. Beat the eggs into the yeast and mix in the flour mixture to a soft dough. Turn on to a lightly floured surface and knead for about 6 minutes or until smooth and no longer sticky. Return to the bowl. Cover with cling film. Leave in a warm place until doubled in bulk.

Knead the dough again until firm. Cut into two equal portions. Cut one of these into two equal pieces and roll these into long strands 30-35 cm / 12-14 inches in length. Arrange the two strands in a cross on a flat surface. Take the two opposite ends of the bottom strand and cross them over the top strand in the centre. Repeat this, using the other strand. Cross each strand alternately, building up the plait vertically, until all the dough is used up. Gather the short ends together and pinch firmly. Lay the challah on its side and place on the prepared baking sheet. Brush with beaten egg. Repeat, using the second portion. Cover with lightly oiled polythene. Leave in a warm place for about 30 minutes or until the dough has doubled. Set the oven at 220°C / 425°F / gas 7. Bake for 35-40 minutes.

MAKES TWO 800 G / 1¾ LB LOAVES

SANDWICHES

The 4th Earl of Sandwich invented the sandwich so that he could eat a light meal without leaving the gaming table. The simple sandwich has gone through many phases, from delicate morsels filled with the thinnest cucumber slices and served to ladies for afternoon tea to today's chunky-cut variety and crunchy, filled baguettes or bread rolls.

Bread Whatever the choice of bread or filling, both must be fresh and in prime condition. A square sandwich loaf which is a day old but not stale is best for thin, dainty sandwiches.

Butter or Margarine It is traditional to spread butter thinly on the bread, both to keep the sandwich together and to prevent moisture from soaking into the bread when filling with moist foods, such as cucumber. Butter should be softened so that it spreads easily. Margarine may be used instead, but only if it is of good quality; strongly flavoured types will ruin the filling. It is not always necessary to spread the bread with either butter or margarine, however. See The Nutritious Sandwich, page 138.

TYPES OF SANDWICHES

Toasted Sandwiches These are usually relatively plain sandwiches which are toasted in a contact grill or sandwich toaster, or under the grill. The filling should be capable of being heated, such as cheese (possibly with onion or tomato slices); ham; tuna with soft cheese; bacon with banana and so on. Salad greens are not suitable.

Double or Triple Decker Sandwiches Three or four slices of bread are sandwiched with one or more fillings. Alternate slices of brown and white bread may be used and the fillings must be complementary. Some suggestions for fillings follow.

Club Sandwiches Three slices of hot, freshly toasted bread are sandwiched with complementary fillings which do not melt. The sandwiches are then cut crossways into four triangles and speared with a cocktail stick holding a garnish of cocktail gherkins and onions. The cocktail stick helps to hold the layers together and the pickles may be replaced by salad ingredients.

Loaf Sandwich The crusts are cut off a sandwich loaf which is then sliced horizontally into four, or more, layers. Each layer is spread with a moist, fairly fine filling (for example, low-fat soft cheese with chopped ham and parsley; finely chopped walnuts with chives and low-fat soft cheese; finely chopped eggs with mayonnaise; chopped chicken with mayonnaise; flaked tuna with mayonnaise or fromage frais), and the loaf is then reassembled, with the layers pressed firmly in place. The loaf is sliced conventionally and the slices cut in half. A Loaf Sandwich is ideal for picnics, served with a salad accompaniment and eaten with a knife and fork.

Chequerboard Sandwiches Made as for the Loaf Sandwich, but with similar-

sized white and wholemeal or granary loaves providing alternate layers of bread which are sandwiched together with a single filling. The reassembled loaf or loaves are cut into thick slices, which are then spread with more filling. The slices are then put back together with every alternate slice inverted to give the reassembled loaf a chequerboard design. The loaf is wrapped and chilled, then sliced before serving.

Pinwheel Sandwiches Thin slices of bread are rolled out between two sheets of greaseproof paper until very thin. When spread with filling, the bread is rolled up, wrapped in greaseproof paper and a polythene bag or foil, then chilled. The roll is sliced into thin pinwheels for serving.

Open Sandwiches These should be decorative and fresh with a generous topping. Open sandwiches are eaten with a knife and fork, so are ideal for smart, light lunches. Rye bread, which is close textured and firm, makes an excellent base, but any bread or split rolls may be used. The main ingredient may be smoked fish, tuna, roast or smoked poultry, cooked ham or roast meat, cured meats, fine slices of pâté, hard-boiled egg or a creamy topping. Salad, fruit, nuts and dressing or relish may be added.

SANDWICH FILLINGS

Avoid very soft ingredients which will soak into the bread; also foods which discolour if the sandwiches are not eaten soon after they are made. Condiments and relishes pep up plain ingredients; for example, mustard, horseradish sauce, cranberry sauce, chutneys and pickles go well with cooked meat and cheese.

Here are a few ideas for savoury and sweet fillings; the possibilities are as broad as you wish. Season savoury mixtures well.

- Tuna, grated lemon rind, chopped hard-boiled egg and low-fat soft cheese or mayonnaise.
- Sardines in oil, mashed with lemon juice and a little garlic, with diced tomato, diced green pepper and lettuce.
- Smoked mackerel, horseradish, diced celery and cucumber slices.
- Peeled, cooked prawns or shrimps with diced avocado and low-fat cheese or mayonnaise, with shredded lettuce.
- Diced salted herring fillet, chopped eating apple, chopped gherkin and chopped onion or spring onion.
- Smoked trout or salmon with a little low-fat soft cheese and chopped fresh dill.
- Diced cooked chicken with grated carrot, chopped walnuts and chopped raisins or sultanas. Low-fat soft cheese or fromage frais may be used to moisten.
- Sliced chicken with diced green or red pepper, chopped pineapple and spring onion. The pepper mixture may be moistened with a little oil and vinegar dressing.
- Chicken with peanut butter and salad greens.

- Smoked or roast turkey with sliced pear and lettuce.
- Roast beef with horseradish, sliced cucumber and red pepper.
- Roast pork with sliced mango and mustard. Add lettuce if liked.
- Sliced cooked sausages with grated apple, soft cheese and mustard.
- Sliced frankfurters or smoked sausage with horseradish sauce and diced avocado.
- Crisp grilled bacon with chopped, ready-to-eat dried apricots and soft cheese. Lettuce may be added if liked.
- Hard-boiled egg with chopped capers, anchovies and cucumber.
- Cold scrambled egg with crispy bacon bits and shredded lettuce.
- Smoked cheese and mashed avocado, with chopped walnuts, peanuts or pecans.
- Goat's milk cheese with chopped dried figs and diced celery.
- Stilton cheese with diced pear and walnuts.
- Roughly chopped button mushrooms with soft cheese, chives and a little horseradish sauce.

THE NUTRITIOUS SANDWICH

The role of sandwiches in the diet is often underestimated: for example, many people rely on them for a light meal at mid-day and an increasing number of children take packed lunches to school. Although there are alternatives to sandwiches, they provide a popular and practical option to plated meals in most busy households.

Sandwiches which make a positive contribution to a balanced diet veer away from the traditional delicate image but are both tasty and satisfying. Cut thick slices of bread, using wholemeal or Granary bread at least some of the time, or chunks of a French-style loaf. There is no need to spread the bread with fat. Include vegetables in the sandwich – sliced cucumber, lettuce, spring onions, grated carrot, sliced tomatoes, shredded cabbage, finely sliced celery and so on. Use a variety of protein-based fillings such as canned tuna, lean poultry or meat and low-fat soft cheese, rather than including chunks of high-fat cheese every day. It is worth remembering that the protein content of the sandwich may not be paramount as this will be balanced by other meals throughout the day. It is perfectly acceptable, therefore to use flavoursome ingredients such as yeast extract and spreads to complement salad ingredients.

Healthy sandwiches should be chunky and well packed with vegetable fillings. Mayonnaise greatly increases the fat content of a packed lunch; reserve it for occasional use.

Crumpets

Crumpets make excellent bases for tasty snacks and starters.
Topped with grilled tomatoes or mushrooms, a poached egg or
toasted cheese, they are also ideal for lunch or supper.

FOOD VALUES	TOTAL	PER CRUMPET (10)
Protein	28g	3g
Carbohydrate	159g	16g
Fat	7g	1g
Fibre	6g	1g
kcals	770	77

200 g / 7 oz strong white
   flour
2.5 ml / ½ tsp salt
2.5 ml / ½ tsp sugar
100 ml / 3½ fl oz milk
10 ml / 2 tsp dried yeast
pinch of bicarbonate of soda
oil for frying

Sift the flour, salt and sugar into a large bowl. Place the milk in a saucepan, add 125 ml / 4 fl oz water and warm gently. The mixture should be just hand-hot. Pour the mixture into a small bowl, sprinkle the dried yeast on top and leave for 10-15 minutes or until frothy.

Add the yeast liquid to the flour and beat to a smooth batter. Cover the bowl with a large lightly oiled polythene bag and leave in a warm place for about 45 minutes or until the batter has doubled. Dissolve the bicarbonate of soda in 15 ml / 1 tbsp warm water; beat into the batter. Cover and leave to rise again for 20 minutes.

Heat a griddle or heavy-bottomed frying pan over medium heat, then grease it when hot. Grease metal crumpet rings, poaching rings or large plain biscuit cutters about 7.5 cm / 3 inches in diameter. Place the rings on the hot griddle, pour a spoonful of batter into each to cover the base thinly and cook until the top is set and the bubbles have burst.

Remove the rings and turn the crumpets over. Cook the other side for 2-3 minutes only, until firm but barely coloured. Cool the crumpets on a wire rack. Serve toasted, with butter.

MAKES 10 TO 12

Bagels

These ring buns are poached in water before baking. The result is a close-textured, moist bread with a deep-golden-coloured crust which is quite thick but not hard. It is worth making a large batch and freezing them: the bagels may be frozen after poaching but before baking – they should be baked after thawing. Alternatively, they may be fully cooked before cooling and freezing.

FOOD VALUES	TOTAL	PER BAGEL
Protein	55g	2g
Carbohydrate	328g	12g
Fat	53g	2g
Fibre	12g	–
kcals	1928	69

oil for greasing
400 g / 14 oz strong white
  flour
5 ml / 1 tsp salt
30 ml / 2 tbsp sugar
50 g / 2 oz margarine
15 g / ½ oz fresh yeast or
  10ml / 2 tsp dried yeast
1 egg, separated
flour for kneading
poppy seeds

Grease 2-3 baking sheets. Sift the flour into a large bowl. Measure 250 ml / 8 fl oz lukewarm water. Put the salt, sugar (reserving 2.5 ml / ½ tsp if using fresh yeast), the margarine and half the water in a saucepan and warm gently until the margarine has melted. Leave until lukewarm.

Blend the fresh yeast to a thin paste with the reserved sugar and the remaining warm water. Set aside in a warm place until frothy – about 5 minutes. Alternatively, sprinkle dried yeast over the warm water and set aside until frothy, then stir well.

Whisk the egg white lightly, then add to the flour with the cooled margarine mixture and the yeast liquid. Mix to a soft dough. Cover the bowl with cling film. Leave in a warm place until the dough has almost doubled in bulk – this will take up to 2 hours, or longer.

Knead the dough again until firm. Cut into 25 g / 1 oz pieces. Roll each piece into a sausage shape 15-20 cm / 6-8 inches in length; then form this into a ring, pinching the ends securely together. Place the

MRS BEETON'S TIP

For a luxurious starter, serve warm bagels with smoked salmon and soured cream, crème fraîche or fromage frais.

rings on a floured surface and leave for 10 minutes or until they begin to rise.

Heat a saucepan of water deep enough to float the bagels, to just below boiling point. Drop in the bagels, a few at a time. Cook them on one side for 2 minutes, then turn them over and cook on the other side for about 2 minutes or until they are light and have risen slightly. Place on the prepared baking sheets. Set the oven at 190°C / 375°F / gas 5.

Beat the egg yolk, brush it over the top surface of the bagels and sprinkle with poppy seeds. Bake for 20-30 minutes, until golden brown and crisp.

MAKES 28

Oatcakes

FOOD VALUES	TOTAL	PER OATCAKE
Protein	14g	1g
Carbohydrate	66g	4g
Fat	50g	3g
Fibre	7g	—
kcals	749	47

oil for greasing
50 g / 2 oz bacon fat or
   dripping
100 g / 4 oz medium
   oatmeal
1.25 ml / ¼ tsp salt
1.25 ml / ¼ tsp bicarbonate
   of soda
fine oatmeal for rolling out

Grease two baking sheets. Set the oven at 160°C / 325°F / gas 3. Melt the bacon or dripping in a large saucepan. Remove from the heat and stir in the dry ingredients, then add enough boiling water to make a stiff dough.

When cool enough to handle, knead the dough thoroughly, then roll out on a surface dusted with fine oatmeal, to a thickness of 5 mm / ¼ inch. Cut into wedge-shaped pieces and transfer to the prepared baking sheets. Bake for 20-30 minutes. Cool on a wire rack.

MAKES ABOUT 16

Rusks

This is an old Suffolk recipe for simple, dry biscuits which are made from a yeasted bread dough. The original recipe used fresh yeast but this version takes advantage of easy-blend yeast. The sugar may be omitted if preferred.

FOOD VALUES	TOTAL	PER RUSK
Protein	38g	3g
Carbohydrate	200g	17g
Fat	33g	3g
Fibre	7g	1g
kcals	1199	100

oil for greasing
225 g / 8 oz strong plain
  flour
15 g / ½ oz easy-blend dried
  yeast
25 g / 1 oz sugar
2.5 ml / ½ tsp salt
25 g / 1 oz butter
75 ml / 3 fl oz milk
1 egg, beaten
flour for kneading

Grease a large baking sheet. Set the oven at 220°C / 425°F / gas 7. Place the flour, yeast, sugar and salt in a mixing bowl. Stir the ingredients together, then make a well in the middle. In a small saucepan, heat the butter and milk together very gently until the butter has melted, then remove the pan from the heat and leave to cool until warm.

Pour the milk mixture into the well in the dry ingredients, add the beaten egg and stir well. Gradually stir in the flour mixture to make a firm dough. Turn the dough out on to a lightly floured surface and knead thoroughly until smooth and elastic. The dough should be kneaded for about 10 minutes.

Place the dough in a clean, lightly floured bowl and cover it with a clean cloth. Set the dough to rise in a warm place until it has doubled in bulk. This may take up to 1½ hours.

Lightly knead the dough again, then divide it into six portions. Shape each portion of dough into an oblong roll measuring about 13 cm / 5 inches in length. Place the rolls on the baking sheet and bake them for about 15-20 minutes, or until they are evenly golden.

Remove the rolls from the oven and reduce the temperature to 180°C / 350°F / gas 4. Using a clean tea-towel to protect your hand, split each roll in half lengthways to make a slim rusk. Return them to the baking sheet, cut side uppermost, and cook for a further 30-40 minutes, or until they are crisp and lightly browned on the cut side. The rusks are ready when they are quite dry. Leave the rusks to cool on a wire rack, then transfer them to an airtight container.

MAKES 12

Simple Crispies

FOOD VALUES	TOTAL	PER CRISPIE
Protein	27g	1g
Carbohydrate	183g	6g
Fat	30g	1g
Fibre	7g	—
kcals	1060	35

oil for greasing
225 g / 8 oz plain flour
good pinch of salt
150 ml / ¼ pint milk
25 g / 1 oz butter

Grease two baking sheets. Set the oven at 190°C / 375°F / gas 5. Sift the flour and salt into a bowl, then make a well in the middle. Heat the milk and butter in a small saucepan until the butter has dissolved, then pour the mixture into the well in the flour. Gradually work the flour into the milk to make a stiff dough. Knead the dough briefly until it is smooth, then roll it out thinly and cut out 7.5 cm / 3 inch crackers.

Place the crackers on the baking sheets and bake them for 6-10 minutes, or until they are golden. Transfer the crackers to a wire rack to cool.

MAKES ABOUT 30

English Muffins

The correct way to serve muffins is to split each one open around the edges almost to the centre. Toast slowly on both sides so that the heat penetrates to the centre, then pull the muffin halves apart, spread with butter, put together again and serve at once.

FOOD VALUES	TOTAL	PER MUFFIN
Protein	65g	3g
Carbohydrate	313g	16g
Fat	42g	2g
Fibre	12g	1g
kcals	1805	90

400 g / 14 oz strong white
  flour
5 ml / 1 tsp salt
25 g / 1 oz butter or
  margarine
225 ml / 7 fl oz milk
10 ml / 2 tsp dried yeast
1 egg
fat for frying

Sift the flour and salt into a large bowl. Rub in the butter or margarine. Place the milk in a saucepan and warm gently. It should be just hand-hot. Pour the milk into a small bowl, sprinkle the dried yeast on top and leave for 10-15 minutes until frothy. Beat in the egg.

Add the yeast liquid to the flour to make a very soft dough. Beat the dough by hand or with a wooden spoon for about 5 minutes until smooth and shiny. Cover the bowl with a large lightly oiled polythene bag and leave in a warm place for 1-2 hours or until doubled in bulk. Beat again lightly.

Roll out on a well floured surface to a thickness of about 1 cm / ½ inch. Using a plain 7.5 cm / 3 inch cutter, cut the dough into rounds. Place the rounds on a floured baking sheet, cover with polythene and leave to rise for about 45 minutes or until light and puffy.

Heat a griddle or heavy-bottomed frying pan, then grease it. Cook the muffins on both sides for about 8 minutes until golden.

MAKES 20

Crisp Crackers

These plain crackers are the ideal accompaniment for cheese. If you use very small cutters to cut the dough, the crackers can be used as a base for making little canapés – top them with piped smooth pâté or cream cheese, olives and parsley.

FOOD VALUES	TOTAL	PER CRACKER
Protein	29g	1g
Carbohydrate	182g	8g
Fat	14g	1g
Fibre	7g	–
kcals	921	38

oil for greasing
225 g / 8 oz plain flour
2.5 ml / ½ tsp salt
about 125 ml / 4 fl oz milk
1 egg yolk, beaten

Grease two baking sheets. Set the oven at 180°C / 350°F / gas 4. Sift the flour and salt into a bowl, then make a well in the middle and add about half the milk. Add the egg yolk to the milk and gradually work in the flour to make a firm dough, adding more milk as necessary.

Turn the dough out on to a lightly floured surface and knead it briefly until it is perfectly smooth. Divide the piece of dough in half and wrap one piece in cling film to prevent it from drying out while you roll out the other piece.

Roll out the dough very thinly and use a 7.5 cm / 3 inch round cutter to stamp out crackers. Gather up the trimmings and re-roll them. Place the crackers on the prepared baking sheets and bake them for 12-18 minutes, until they are golden. Transfer the crackers to a wire rack to cool.

MAKES ABOUT 24

Caraway Crackers

Originally, these simple biscuits were sweetened with 50 g / 2 oz caster sugar but the flavour of the caraway seeds makes such an excellent savoury cracker that the sugar is omitted in this recipe. However, if you particularly like the flavour of caraway you may like to try the old recipe and add the sugar to the flour. If you are making the savoury crackers try using brown flour instead of white.

FOOD VALUES	TOTAL	PER CRACKER
Protein	29g	1g
Carbohydrate	175g	6g
Fat	50g	2g
Fibre	7g	—
kcals	1224	41

oil for greasing
50 g / 2 oz butter
225 g / 8 oz plain flour
30 ml / 2 tbsp caraway seeds
good pinch of salt
1 egg, beaten
milk for glazing

Grease two baking sheets. Set the oven at 180°C / 350°F / gas 4. Place the butter in a bowl and beat it until it is very soft. Gradually beat in the flour, caraway seeds and salt until the ingredients are thoroughly mixed.

Add the beaten egg and mix well to make a firm dough. Knead the dough briefly on a floured surface, then roll it out thinly and cut out 5 cm / 2 inch circles.

Place the crackers on the baking sheets and brush them with a little milk, then bake them for about 12-15 minutes. Transfer the crackers to a wire rack to cool.

MAKES ABOUT 30

SPREADS AND RELISHES

SERVING SPREADS AND RELISHES

The variety of recipes in this chapter illustrate the versatility of these simple, well flavoured savoury mixtures. Spreads may be used to flavour elegant canapés as well as providing nutritious fillings for sandwiches. Home-made chutneys and pickles are the ideal accompaniments for a simple bread and cheese lunch – and they often replace butter as they are moist and well flavoured.

Sprat Paste

Serve this paste with wholemeal toast for lunch or use it as a sandwich filling, adding sliced cucumber, shredded lettuce and spring onions, if liked.

FOOD VALUES	TOTAL
Protein	46g
Carbohydrate	—
Fat	37g
Fibre	—
kcals	521

450 g / 1 lb sprats, cleaned
10 ml / 2 tsp butter
pinch of cayenne pepper
black pepper
1.25 ml / ¼ tsp ground
   mace
5 ml / 1 tsp anchovy essence
15 ml / 1 tbsp lemon juice

Set the oven at 180°C / 350°F / gas 4. Place the sprats on a large sheet of foil supported on a baking sheet. Dot the fish with butter and fold the foil over to make a loose parcel. Bake for 10-15 minutes.

While still warm, remove the heads, tails, skin and backbones from the fish. Pound the flesh well in a mortar, then rub through a sieve into a small bowl.

Add cayenne, black pepper and mace to taste, then beat in the anchovy essence and lemon juice. Turn into small pots. Cover and refrigerate until the paste is firm.

MAKES ABOUT 450 G / 1 LB

Anchovy Relish

Spread this well-spiced relish thinly on fingers of toast or bread and butter; or use it to flavour canapés. Spread on rounds of toast and topped with poached eggs or grilled mushrooms it makes an interesting starter.

FOOD VALUES	TOTAL	PER PORTION
Protein	13g	1g
Carbohydrate	—	—
Fat	74g	6g
Fibre	—	—
kcals	688	57

1 (50 g / 2 oz) can anchovies
2.5 ml / ½ tsp allspice
1.25 ml / ¼ tsp grated nutmeg
1.25 ml / ¼ tsp ground mace
1.25 ml / ¼ tsp ground ginger
pinch of ground cloves
2.5 ml / ½ tsp Worcestershire sauce
50 g / 2 oz butter, softened
freshly ground black pepper

Pound the anchovies to a paste with the oil from the can. Alternatively, process them in a food processor until smooth. Add the spices individually, pounding in each addition, then mix in the Worcestershire sauce.

Add the butter and work it with the spiced anchovies until thoroughly combined. Add pepper to taste. Transfer to a small pot, cover and chill until ready to use. The paste keeps for up to 4 days in the refrigerator.

MAKES ABOUT 75 G / 3 OZ, ENOUGH TO
SPREAD THINLY ON ABOUT 12 TOAST SLICES

Simple Soft Cheese

Strictly speaking this is not a cheese at all – it is strained yogurt which becomes thick and similar in texture to a soft cheese. It can be used as a low-fat substitute for soft cheese in many recipes or flavoured to serve as a spread.

FOOD VALUES	TOTAL	PER 25 g / 1 oz
Protein	56g	6g
Carbohydrate	83g	9g
Fat	9g	1g
Fibre	–	–
kcals	618	69

1.1 *litres / 2 pints plain yogurt or low-fat fromage frais*
30 *ml / 2 tbsp lemon juice*

Have ready a large piece of double-thick scalded muslin. Put the yogurt or fromage frais in a bowl and stir in the lemon juice. Pour the mixture into the muslin and gather up the corners, then hang the yogurt or fromage frais overnight in a cool place.

Discard the liquid, then squeeze the muslin lightly. Use a spatula to scrape the 'cheese' into a bowl. Cover and chill.

MAKES ABOUT 225 G / 8 OZ

VARIATIONS

- Add salt and pepper to taste. Mix in chopped parsley, a little chopped fresh tarragon, some chopped fresh thyme and a little crushed garlic (if liked). Press neatly into a dish and chill until ready to serve with crackers or crusty bread.
- Mix 50 g / 2 oz finely chopped walnuts and 45 ml / 3 tbsp snipped chives into the cheese.
- Finely chop seeded red pepper, then add it to the cheese with 30 ml / 2 tbsp grated onion and salt and pepper to taste.

Potted Cheese

Serve this creamy potted cheese with crackers or bread, celery sticks, radishes, apple and chicory leaves for a light lunch or supper.

FOOD VALUES	TOTAL	PER 25 g / 1 oz
Protein	128g	7g
Carbohydrate	7g	–
Fat	156g	9g
Fibre	–	–
kcals	1993	111

450 g / 1 lb Cheddar or
 Cheshire cheese, finely
 grated
100 g / 4 oz low-fat soft
 cheese
salt
pinch of ground mace
30-45 ml / 2-3 tbsp cream
 sherry or tawny port

Pound about one third of the grated cheese with the low-fat soft cheese until smooth, or process in a blender or food processor. Add the remaining cheese with salt, mace and sherry or port. Pound to a smooth paste. Turn into small pots. Cover and chill for at least an hour before serving.

MAKES ABOUT 450 G / 1 LB

NUTRITION NOTE

The firm types of low-fat soft cheese are a good substitute for butter in mixtures such as potted cheese or fish pâtés and other spreads which usually rely on butter for their texture and richness.

Pickled Onions

This is a recipe for onions without tears. Soaking the unskinned onions in brine makes them easy to peel. Since the only ingredients actually *eaten* in this recipe are the onions, a food value chart is not necessary.

450 g / 1 lb salt
1.4 kg / 3 lb pickling onions
2.25 litres / 4 pints cold
  Spiced Vinegar, see Mrs
  Beeton's Tip
5 ml / 1 tsp mustard seeds
  (optional)

Dissolve half the salt in 2 litres / 3½ pints of water in a large bowl. Add the onions. Set a plate inside the bowl to keep the onions submerged, weighting the plate with a jar filled with water. Do not use a can as the salt water would corrode it. Leave for 24 hours.

Drain and skin the onions and return them to the clean bowl. Make up a fresh solution of brine, using the rest of the salt and a further 2 litres / 3½ pints water. Pour it over the onions, weight as before and leave for a further 24 hours.

Drain the onions, rinse them thoroughly to remove excess salt, and drain again. Pack into wide-mouthed jars. Cover with cold spiced vinegar, adding a few mustard seeds to each jar, if liked. Cover with vinegar-proof lids. Label and store in a cool, dark place. Keep for at least 1 month before using.

MAKES ABOUT 1.4 KG / 3 LB

MRS BEETON'S TIP

Spiced vinegar is the basis for a large number of chutneys, pickles and relishes. To make 1 litre / 1¾ pints you will need 7g / ¼ oz each of the following spices: cloves, allspice berries, broken cinnamon sticks, and bruised fresh root ginger, plus 1 litre / 1¾ pints white or malt vinegar. Fold the spices in a clean cloth. Beat them lightly with a rolling pin to release all the flavour, then transfer them to a large jug with the vinegar. Mix well, pour the mixture into a 1.1 litre / 2 pint bottle and seal tightly. Shake daily for 1 month, then store in a cool dry place for at least 1 month more before straining out the spices and returning the spiced vinegar to the clean bottle.

Pickled Beetroot

1.4 *kg* / 3 *lb beetroot*
600-750 *ml* / 1-1¼ *pints*
 Spiced Vinegar, *see* Mrs
 Beeton's Tip opposite
15-20 *g* / ½-¾ *oz salt*

Set the oven at 180°C / 350°F / gas 4. Wash the beetroot thoroughly but gently, taking care not to break the skin. Place in a roasting tin and bake for 45-60 minutes or until tender. Cool, then skin and cube. Pour the spiced vinegar into a saucepan, add the salt and bring to the boil.

Meanwhile, pack the beetroot cubes into wide-mouthed jars. Cover with boiling vinegar and put on vinegar-proof covers. Seal, label, cool, then store in a cool, dark place for 3 months before eating.

MAKES ABOUT 1.4 KG / 3 LB.

NUTRITION NOTE

Food values are not included for Pickled Onions or Pickled Beetroot as they do not contain significant quantities of these nutrients.

Bread and Butter Pickles

FOOD VALUES	TOTAL
Protein	32g
Carbohydrate	457g
Fat	5g
Fibre	30g
kcals	1887

1.5 kg / 3¼ lb large
cucumbers
1.5 kg / 3¼ lb small onions,
thinly sliced
75 g / 3 oz cooking salt
375 ml / 13 fl oz white wine
vinegar or distilled
vinegar
300 g / 11 oz soft light
brown sugar
2.5 ml / ½ tsp turmeric
2.5 ml / ½ tsp ground cloves
15 ml / 1 tbsp mustard seeds
2.5 ml / ½ tsp celery seeds

Wash the cucumbers but do not peel them. Slice thinly. Layer with the onions and salt in a large bowl (see Mrs Beeton's Tip). Cover with a plate weighted down with a jar filled with water. Leave for 3 hours.

Rinse the vegetables thoroughly, drain and place in a large saucepan. Add the vinegar and bring to the boil. Lower the heat and simmer for 10-12 minutes or until the cucumber slices begin to soften.

Add the remaining ingredients, stirring over low heat until the sugar has dissolved. Bring to the boil, then remove from the heat. Turn the contents of the pan carefully into a large heatproof bowl. Leave until cold. Spoon into clean jars, seal with vinegar-proof covers, label and store in a cool dark place.

MAKES ABOUT 3.25 KG / 7 LB

MRS BEETON'S TIP

To make the pickle especially crisp and crunchy, cover the final layer of cucumber with about 600 ml / 1 pint crushed ice before leaving the salted mixture to stand.

Sweetcorn Relish

FOOD VALUES	TOTAL
Protein	21g
Carbohydrate	204g
Fat	11g
Fibre	16g
kcals	943

2 green peppers, seeded and diced
2 large carrots, diced
2 large onions, chopped
6 celery sticks, diced
salt
2 garlic cloves, crushed
30 ml / 2 tbsp mustard powder
5 ml / 1 tsp turmeric
15 ml / 1 tbsp cornflour
600 ml / 1 pint white vinegar
900 g / 2 lb frozen sweetcorn, thawed
100 g / 4 oz sugar

Place the peppers, carrots, chopped onion and celery in a bowl, sprinkling each layer with a little salt. Sprinkle more salt on top of the vegetables, cover the bowl and leave them to stand overnight.

Next day, drain, rinse, drain again and dry the vegetables, then place them in a large saucepan with the garlic. In a cup, blend the mustard, turmeric and cornflour to a paste with a little of the vinegar. Pour the rest of the vinegar into the pan and bring the vegetable mixture to the boil. Lower the heat and cover the pan, then simmer the mixture for 5 minutes. Add the sweetcorn and cook, covered, for a further 5 minutes. Stir in the sugar and cook gently, stirring, until it has dissolved.

Spoon a little of the hot liquid into the mustard mixture, then stir the thin paste into the relish. Add 5 ml / 1 tsp salt and stir well. Bring to the boil, stirring all the time, then lower the heat and simmer steadily for 5 minutes without a lid on the pan. Pot and cover at once, then cool, wipe the jars, label and store for at least a week. The relish will keep for 6-9 months.

MAKES ABOUT 2.25 KG / 5 LB

155

Green Tomato Chutney

Aside from its obvious uses, as an accompaniment for bread and cheese or curried foods, green tomato chutney can be used instead of a garnish on cold platters that include sliced pâté or pork cheese.

FOOD VALUES	TOTAL
Protein	38g
Carbohydrate	913g
Fat	9g
Fibre	40g
kcals	3660

450 g / 1 lb cooking apples
450 g / 1 lb onions, chopped
2 kg / 4½ lb green tomatoes, roughly chopped
450 g / 1 lb sultanas
15 g / ½ oz salt
1.25 ml / ¼ tsp cayenne pepper
15 ml / 1 tbsp mustard seeds
1 cm / ½ inch fresh root ginger, bruised
750 ml / 1¼ pints malt vinegar
450 g / 1 lb demerara sugar

Peel, core and chop the apples. Put them in a large saucepan or preserving pan with the onions, tomatoes and sultanas. Stir in the salt and cayenne. Tie the mustard seeds and root ginger in a muslin bag and add to the pan with just enough of the vinegar to cover. Bring to simmering point and simmer for 20 minutes.

Meanwhile combine the remaining vinegar and the sugar in a second pan, stirring constantly over gentle heat until the sugar has dissolved. Add the vinegar mixture to the large saucepan or preserving pan and boil steadily until the chutney reaches the desired consistency. Remove the spice bag.

Pour the chutney into warm clean jars and cover with vinegar-proof lids. When cool, wipe the jars, label and store in a cool dry place.

MAKES ABOUT 3 KG / 6½ LB

MRS BEETON'S TIP

When filling jars, stand them on a sheet of paper to catch any drips.

Gooseberry Chutney

FOOD VALUES	TOTAL
Protein	64g
Carbohydrate	1053g
Fat	26g
Fibre	68g
kcals	4437

450 g / 1 lb soft light brown sugar
1.5 litres / 2¾ pints vinegar
450 g / 1 lb onions, finely chopped
675 g / 1½ lb seedless raisins
50 g / 2 oz mustard seeds, gently bruised
50 g / 2 oz ground allspice
50 g / 2 oz salt
2 kg / 4½ lb gooseberries, topped and tailed

Put the sugar in a large saucepan or preserving pan with half the vinegar. Heat gently, stirring, until the sugar dissolves, then bring to the boil and boil for a few minutes until syrupy. Add the onions, raisins, spices and salt.

Bring the remaining vinegar to the boil in a second pan, add the gooseberries, lower the heat and simmer until tender. Stir the mixture into the large saucepan or preserving pan, cooking until the mixture thickens to the desired consistency. Pour the chutney into warm clean jars and cover with vinegar-proof lids. When cool, wipe the jars, label and store in a cool dry place.

MAKES ABOUT 3 KG / 6½ LB

MRS BEETON'S TIP

Allspice is a berry grown in the Caribbean area. Its name derives from the flavour, which suggests a blend of cinnamon, nutmeg and cloves. It is added whole to pickles, chutneys, stews and marinades, while the ground form is used in all foods, especially cakes and puddings.

INDEX